Memories of
Enderby

Memories of
Enderby

John and Susan Crofts

J.R.Crofts

S.Crofts.

TEMPUS

For my brother, Guy

Frontispiece *Some Enderby residents on holiday in Rhyl, early 1920s.*

First published 2004

Tempus Publishing Limited
The Mill, Brimscombe Port,
Stroud, Gloucestershire, GL5 2QG

British Library Cataloguing in Publication Data.
A catalogue record for this book is available from the British Library.

ISBN 0 7524 3373 3

Typesetting and origination by Tempus Publishing Limited
Printed in Great Britain

Contents

	List of Contributors	6
	Introduction and Acknowledgements	7
one	Schooldays	9
two	Growing up	21
three	Shops and Businesses	31
four	Working Life	45
five	Worship	65
six	Wartime	75
seven	Sport	87
eight	Village Life	95
nine	Village Characters	119

List of Contributors

Mavis Almond, Graham Anderson, Ray Bingley, Eileen Briers, Derek Brooks, Molly Broomhall and Joyce Turner, Ted Brown, Barry Bryan, Christine Bryan, Edna Burgess, Stuart Buzzard, Jean Carter, Arthur Cherry, Nigel Cooper, Roy Coulson, Mary Cox, Joyce Fawell, Lenny Fawell, Herbert Gilliver, Clive Hall, Norma Hall, Frank Humphrey, Sadie Jayes, John Lane, Pam Lawrance (*née* Preston), Laurence Lilley, David North, Judith North, Mark Postlethwaite, Beryl Seymour, Garry Sleath, Alan Smith, Jenny Smith, Jeff Steer, Ken Thomas, Sheila Thorpe, Claire Timmins, Doris Webster, Laurence (Curly) West, Dorothy Williams, Ernie Yeomanson and Arnold Young.

And two gentlemen and one lady who wished to remain anonymous.

Enderby orchestra in the early 1900s.

Introduction and Acknowledgements

This book is not intended to be a history of Enderby, more a record of the memories of people living there over the past ninety years or so. There is therefore information from a wide age range, reflecting different aspects of village life. I have edited the interviews where necessary to avoid repetition and for ease of understanding for the reader, without changing the sense of what was said.

It has been my privilege to interview people whose ages range from early forties to a centenarian. I have tried to include a broad variety of village life and events as seen through the eyes of those who were there. The stories you will read are personal memories of village people and, as with all memories, some facts may have been blurred with time. I have done my best to ensure that names, places and dates are correct, but where there are errors, I apologise. Contributors have been very generous with their time and their memories, but, sadly, I have not been able to include all the material from each interview.

My grateful thanks go to all the contributors for their patience, enthusiasm and willingness to let me into their homes, to share their memories with me and my tape recorder and to dig out their photographs for me. A few people have wished to remain anonymous and, of course, I have respected their wishes. Special thanks go to Arnold Young for all his help and support. Finally, I am grateful to my wife for transforming the spoken word into print.

The writing of this book has opened my eyes to the richness and diversity of the Enderby community into which I moved as a newly wed some thirty-odd years ago. Without the co-operation of the residents of the village, this book could not have been written, and the wealth of stories and information would have been lost to future generations

John Crofts
Enderby, 2004

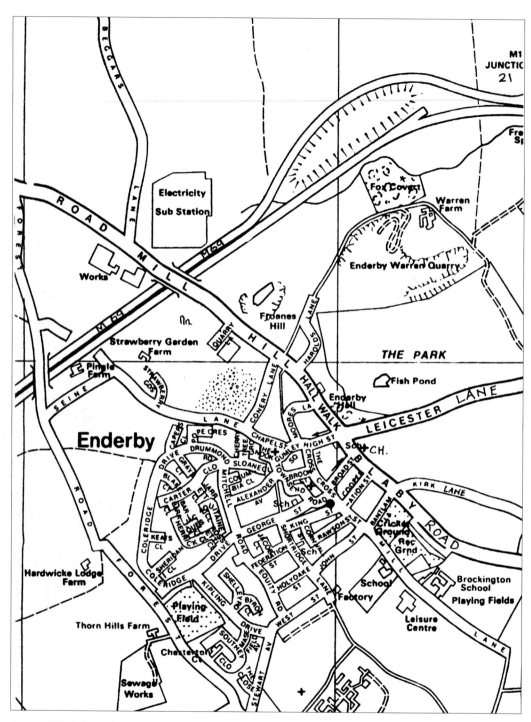

A map of Enderby in the 1980s.

one
Schooldays

I loved school

My first school was at Townsend Road, Enderby. The headmistress was Miss Moore, a very firm lady, but very fair. From the moment I was at that school until the moment I left, I adored it, and never wanted to be ill or miss it. All the teachers were very nice.

We played skipping and all those things you never see these days. We played a lot of snobs. We did reading, writing and arithmetic, and we always had P.E. The lady that took P.E. was also interested in the theatrical side, and we had a lot of plays, very nice plays. Mrs Harris, she was up to all these things, she was very good.

Mary Cox

Twopenny magazines

You went to the primary school, Townsend Road, for a start off, and then you went to the big school when you were eight. Mrs Pritchard was the head person at the primary, and then there was Mrs Cutler and Lizzie Harris; they were teachers there. Then when you got round to there (the school opposite the church), there was Mr Capers, and when we was old enough, it was Mr Jackson, the headmaster. He got so that he didn't teach, and we were left for hours doing nothing. We used to take twopenny magazines and read. Mr Jackson was too busy seeing to the other classes and he left us, and this is something that I always regret. We used to go down the recreation ground – I don't know whether there's still a swing there – on a Thursday afternoon, and play cricket and football and other games like that. And we used to go – I think it was on a Monday – from the big school round to the primary school for cookery lessons.

D.L.

Townsend Road school, 1917.

Children of Townsend Road school dressed for a fête at Enderby Hall, 1936.

My long name

Miss Billingham was my first teacher. She used to tear up a sheet of paper lengthways, and we had to write our names on it. My name was Christine Woofenden, and I couldn't get all my name on one side of the paper, so I'd write Christine on one side, and Woofenden on the other. She was always telling me off for this. When I told my mum, she said that she had been told off too. Miss Billingham said 'Fancy giving the child a long name like that.'

Christine Bryan

Scarlet Fever

I went to the primary school. Miss Billingham, I think, was the teacher. She was such a small lady, not much bigger than some of the children really, the older ones. While I was there, I had scarlet fever. There was an epidemic. My brother had it before me, and he was dying to tell me you got an injection in your bottom. My mother was there and kept shutting him up, because I'd got to go in, and it was the first time I'd been away from home. You had to go to the Blaby Isolation Hospital in Hospital Lane, and in there, the windows were all done up with stuff from the war, sandbags. Your parents could only look through the window at you, you weren't allowed to meet them at all. They got me dressing some little lad, and I put his trousers on the wrong way round and his shoes on the wrong feet.

Joyce Fawell

Knuckles – Ouch!

In Townsend Road, Miss Moore was the head teacher. I particularly remember Gladys Clarke who was one of the young teachers – she happened to live next door. We had a

Enderby school football team, 1923/1924.

teacher who had come from London, a Miss Gardner, she was a very good teacher, and Miss Finucane. Miss Gardner smoked, which at that time was unusual for a woman. It's amazing what sticks in your mind! But they were very strict, and you got the cane and often got rapped over the knuckles with a six-sided heavy pencil or bashed on the knuckles with a ruler by the teachers. That's what they were used to.

During the war, at the junior school, we learned to do knitting. We knitted small squares to be made into blankets for the soldiers. My father went to school in Enderby, and he said that when the fox hunt came round, they always took a day off school. They knew they would get the cane the next day for having the day off.

Arnold Young

Cocoa at school

I went to Townsend Road school. Miss Moore was the headmistress there. One step out of line and bang, bang, bang on your knuckles with a thick pencil. I had that many a time. Then there was a Miss Johnson, she'd throw chalk at you. She'd hit you on the knuckles with a blackboard pointer as well. It was mainly the three Rs and you would chant your tables. I can remember my mother bringing me a mug of cocoa down at playtime on cold days because we only lived about three or four hundred yards away. She'd come down with a steaming hot jug of cocoa for me and my brother. In the classroom there were double seats, all set in rows, with lift-up lids, and the teacher stood at the front.

Jeff Steer

Playtime snack

At morning playtime, my mother used to come down to the school with two rounds of fried bread with egg and bacon in between. All the kids used to follow me around saying 'Giz a bit of fried bread, Ern.'

Ernie Yeomanson

Having a nap

We moved from our house in Federation Street when my auntie died, because my grandmother didn't want strangers in the yard. There were only the two houses in the yard, so we moved to the house next door to my grandmother. I went to the junior school at Townsend Road, and my teacher was a Miss Dixon. I remember in the afternoons they used to put camp beds out and we'd have a nap in the afternoons. We used to go home for our dinner, then back to school for a sleep, which wasn't bad at all.

Enderby school, late 1900s.

There was no whistle blown to get us into school. One of the teachers had a dustpan and banged it with a hand-brush. By the time I got to the top class with Mrs Cutler, the war was on. When the sirens went, we all used to run home – those that lived near the school went home, and they took somebody who lived further away with them. I used to take a lad called Barry with me, his mum lived in High Street and they thought it was too far for him to go home. Later, when there was talk of them machine-gunning the streets, we had to stay in school and go under the desks when the sirens went. Of course, the teachers used to say that was a good time for the gas-mask drill, so we sat under the desks with our masks on until the all-clear sounded. Sometimes, there was no milk for the children to drink, so you had a choice of either an Ovaltine tablet or a Horlicks tablet. You couldn't have both.

Stuart Buzzard

the life out of us, he did, because if you had to have any teeth out, you had a sweet when you came round. I had to have one out, and I played up, so I didn't get my sweet.

Laurence Lilley

Happy Days

I started school at Townsend Road. I loved it there. There was Miss Dixon in the first class, and then Miss Sharpe – the Misses Sharpe lived in the big house round the Hardwicke – and then Miss Harris, who became the farmer's wife in Thurlaston. I had Mrs Harris, who lived in Federation Street, and Mrs Birch, who was Frew West's mother. The top class was Mrs Cutler. She seemed so elderly to me, though I don't suppose she was that old. Miss Moore was the headmistress. She came from Hinckley. I think she used to cycle to school.

Eileen Briers

No teacher's pet

I went to Townsend Road school. I can remember the headmistress, Miss Alcock, her name was, and I started off in her class. She took the very first juniors and she lived down Seine Lane near us, at the farm further down where the nursery (Hawgrip) is now. When we came out of school, my sister and I some-times saw Miss Alcock, the headmistress. She wouldn't let us walk with her. She didn't want us to think we were getting better treatment than the other kids. I can understand it now, but we had to walk home by ourselves. It was very strict at Townsend Road School. We had a slate to write on, with a wooden frame round it. Next to us was the cooking area, where the children learned to cook. When the dentist came, he used that room. He used to frighten

Townsend Road School, 1999.

White Horse

There was a game called white horse. One boy would stoop down next to a wall with his hands against the wall, another boy would run up and jump on his back, and then another would do the same. We'd try to pile them up, as many as we could, until the pile collapsed.

Ray Bingley

Ticked off for playing tick

We used to go down to the 'breach' and take a snack with us, probably a bottle of cold tea as there was no pop for us in those days. Usually, when we wanted to play, we went into the first field, but on this particular day we went into the cornfield and played tick. We didn't think Miss Sharpe, our teacher, could see us from her window, but next morning, in school, we had to stand in front of the class, and we got the ruler across our fingers. It was a bad thing to do, but we didn't think about it, we were just having fun. We didn't do it again, though!

Pam Lawrance (*née* Preston)

School photo

I went to Townsend Road school. There was recently a picture in the *Leicester Mercury* of my class. I wasn't on it and I had to think a long way back, but eventually I realised that just about that time I'd have been in hospital in Hinckley with scarlet fever. I sat next to Claire Timmins in school. Doreen Brookes was top of the class.

Ted Brown

Learning a poem

I learned this poem when I was five or six years old. It was called *Toothache*:

Measles, they're horrid, and mumps are rather bad,
Scarlet fever's dreadful, but toothache drives you mad.
It takes you and it shakes you, til your face is twice the size,
Your cheeks are round the corner and you haven't any eyes.
If you were not so little, I'd go and pull it out,
I'd lay it on the table and turn it round about.
I'd smother it with toffee and sticky currant cake,
Then for twenty hours, I'd stand and watch it ache.

Mavis Almond

Class 3B, Enderby church school, 1946. Nigel Cooper is third from right, middle row

Going to school with Grandad

I remember, me grandad used to take me to school because me mam was at work. In them days, I only had to go from the 'King Bill' in Shortridge Lane round to 'Backside' – that's what we called Townsend Road, where the school was. It wasn't as big as it is now, of course, and the cinema was there as well, the Enderby Picture House. We used to go there quite a lot. In school, there was Miss Sharpe, she later married and became Mrs Ashmore. There was also Mrs Hill who came from Kirby Muxloe, Miss Moore, who was the head-mistress, and Miss Finucane. During the war, we had to get under the desks when the sirens went. The siren was at Empire Stone.

Nigel Cooper

The Ice Queen

When we were in the first class, we used to have a rest every afternoon. They used to lay out rush mats on the floor. I never went to sleep, but some children used to go off fast asleep. If they were still asleep after half-an-hour, they'd leave them, covered with blankets made of knitted squares. One year, we did a Christmas play, *The Ice Queen*. We had lovely dresses made, our parents had to get them made.

Eileen Briers

Hurrah for the holidays

I didn't want school. I wanted to be out and about, doing something. In July, the school would close for the holidays. We only had about two weeks then. I remember, we had this little service to finish school for the holiday, and some of them were crying because they were leaving school. Not me!

Sadie Jayes

Thrown out of the school choir!

I was born in August, so I was only just five when I started at Townsend Road school. My first teacher was Miss Aston. The school building seemed so big when you were only three-feet-tall. It had such high ceilings. I remember being thrown out of the choir. It

Danemill school staff, 1978. Miss Aston is second left, front row.

was devastating for a five year old. We joined the choir and all stood there, singing, when the teacher walked along the line and said someone was singing out of tune. She went down the line of these poor little five year olds, all singing their hearts out, and stopped when she got to me. She said, 'Right, you don't have to come back again'. Imagine, I could have been an opera singer now!

Mark Postlethwaite

Playground games

I started school at Townsend Road primary school when I was five, and I can remember to this day going there on my first day with my mother. I can remember some of the antics we got up to towards the end of primary school. In the playground at the back, when it was winter, we used to make long slides. 'Keep the kettle boiling,' we sang, going round and round on these slides, and hitting the wall at the bottom. We played the normal games of ball, skipping and football. I remember the toilets were outside, and they used to freeze up in winter. There was Mr Moore

who was there, and the headmistress was Mrs Young. She only lived across the road, where the houses are now, at the back of Kwik-Save. Then there was Mr West who came. I think he was headmaster, and his wife, who was Fru Birch in those days. I can't remember there being any strict discipline in the primary school, it was later, when we went to secondary school where it was far different to what it is nowadays.

Derek Brooks

Taking the eleven-plus

I remember from the little school you could take the eleven-plus exam, and if you passed, you went on to Hinckley. I wasn't quite good enough for that. I remember when I had an interview and they asked me a lot of questions like, 'If you had a ton of coal and a ton of feathers, which would be the heaviest?' I didn't like school – I just didn't enjoy it. I always did well, but it used to worry me, because you always had to try so hard to get good marks.

Joyce Fawell

A lady on a motorbike

There was Mr Jackson and Mr Capers, and there was a lady, Miss Hall, who came all the way from Broughton Astley on a motorbike. She used to dress in leathers and she did it every day, going backwards and forwards. She married the chap who came to look after the carpentry shop. Once they were married, they lived in Mr Gittings' house on Blaby Road.

Laurence Lilley

Derek Brooks' mother and grandmother, 21 King Street, 1908.

The vicar in school

It was called the big school by the local kids and it was round near the church. I remember how the vicar used to call over and go through all the classes and then just have a word with the teacher, all in his white robes. Of course, there (at the church school) they had classes that were only divided by a sliding partition. I didn't used to get into much trouble at school, but my dad said that when he was at school, he used to get the cane almost every day with Mr Jackson, who was the headmaster then. He used to come up from Beggars Lane every day, my dad did, and he'd walk along there to get to school.

Joyce Fawell

Walking round for school

Mr Turk was the headmaster at the church school. We used to have about thirty people in a class. We used to do art at the top chapel, and we'd go down Mill Lane to some other buildings. The dinner centre was next to the King Bill pub – that's where they did cooking and woodwork, and science was taught upstairs. You did a lot of walking from one place to another.

Christine Bryan

Secondary school

I went to the school in Townsend Road to start with. I took the eleven-plus exam and got an A3, so I didn't get into the grammar school. Instead, I went to the school opposite the church. Some of the teachers I remember were Mr Insley and his wife, Mr Capers and Mr Atter. I was in Mr Atter's class, then I went into Mrs Insley's class. Different teachers took you for different subjects, like Mr Insley took us all for woodwork. The woodwork place was next to the King William, and that was what they called the 'centre'. You went there for science and woodwork, and the girls went there for cookery. People used to come to the school from different villages like Thurlaston, Croft, Narborough, Blaby and Whetstone. They all went to Enderby School. It was the main centre, and, of course, they stayed there for dinner rather than going home for it. There was a room at the centre where they had their dinner. At one time, when the classes got too big, they would take classes in the Co-operative Hall.

B.T.

The old church school, 2000.

The hunt comes to Enderby

I can remember the hunt coming to the village when I was at school. It must have been playtime, because we were all hanging over the railings. The hunt came up Leicester Lane with all the dogs and everything, and they were milling around at the crossroads for quite a while. I don't know if they were waiting for someone else to join them, but eventually they galloped off up Hall Walk.

David North

Views change

I went to Townsend Road school as a junior, and then as a senior. When I was about twelve years old, I went to the school opposite the church. I left at fourteen. Our class teacher throughout the main part of my education was Miss Hall, and Mr Jackson was the headmaster. He lived at the top end of what is now Alexander Avenue. Another character I remember was Arthur Capers. I didn't like him much in those days because not many children do like their teachers to that extent, but later in life, I came to enjoy his company,

and I admired a lot about him. Arthur was Arthur's man, but he was a knowledgeable man of the village, and a gentleman who devoted his life to Enderby.

Frank Humphrey

Childhood

My parents lived in Havelock Yard. Mother used to work round at Dan Burgess's, on the winding. She had to bring us up on our two own, me and my brother. It used to be where the children's day nursery is now, near the corner of George Street. It was an old wooden shack really.

My granddad were a quarry worker, liked his pint. Every night my grandma would trot round with a little bag. Inside were a quart bottle and a pint bottle from the Nag's Head, and he'd sip it from the bottle.

There were seven children and my grandma and granddad in a little cottage, one room downstairs and a tiny little kitchen, and two small bedrooms. They used to divide the kids, the girls from the boys, with sheets strung down the middle of the bedroom, and they were crammed into a little space.

Jeff Steer

The headmaster's house, Hall Walk, 1999.

Down by the river

In the school holidays, we sometimes went for a picnic. We lived in Mill Lane, and we were allowed to go down Mill Lane and through the fields, over what is now the dual carriageway. From there, we went down a passage at the side of Enderby House, and on to the river. In those times, we used to paddle, and all the boys would swim. I remember we used to take a bottle of cold tea or kali water and some sandwiches, and have a thoroughly good time. We used to fish or swim in the water.

Mavis Almond

Brockington School – how it has grown

When I first came to Enderby, Brockington school was only five years old. It had been erected in the late fifties and was obviously a very new building then. Since then it has had many extensions. During the early part of my time there, a second science laboratory was built, and on top of that, a domestic science room, and the gym was built. In subsequent years, we had extensions in almost every direction. The community college was enlarged with the Drummond Centre. The main thing with the building was that these extensions enlarged the capacity of the school but the size of the corridors remained the same. This has been a constant problem.

In the late fifties, new schools, including Brockington, were being built with pre-stressed concrete held together with wires. This was known as an 'intergrid' structure, and over the last fifteen years this intergrid structure has been failing.

The school catered for a large area. As well as Enderby, students came from Narborough, Thurlaston, Huncote, Whetstone, Cosby and, of course, Broughton Astley. It wasn't until the late sixties that students from Broughton Astley and Cosby went to the new Thomas Estley school for their high-school education.

John Lane

School trips

I started as head of science in the school. I was full-time and I had two part-time teachers with me. The school organised a lot of trips in those days, far more than nowadays with the pressures of the National Curriculum. I was involved in a lot of canal trips. We would hire two boats and I and two other teachers would take groups of students out. We usually went on the Oxford canal as it was fairly close by. Each boat would take about twelve children on the outward journey, then a colleague would meet us with another group of children and we would swap for the return journey. That way, we could give forty-eight children the chance of some days away on the boats. Of course, the boats in those days were not of the standard they are today. They were ex-coal carrying boats with canvas tops, and we literally camped under the canvas. We had some memorable times, especially going through the Braunstone Tunnel and the Blisworth Tunnel, which at that time was one of the longest on the canal network. We did these trips for a number of years until, sadly, it became one of those activities that priced itself out of the market.

John Lane

John Lane, head of science for many years at Brockington College.

School trip in the snow

We once went on a trip to the railway museum at Crich with our teacher Mr Crane. It was in April, and it snowed and snowed. The drifts actually came up to Mr Crane's waist. I'm amazed they didn't cancel the trip

Brockington College, Mill Lane, 2000.

because the conditions were awful, but the atmosphere in that Peak District setting was fantastic.

Mark Postlethwaite

Brockington PTA

There was a very active parents' association at Brockington, and, of course, with the swimming pool there was always a need to raise money. We had a Saturday afternoon fête in the summer where the girls did a fashion show of the clothes they had made themselves in needlework lessons, under the guidance of teachers like Margaret Cooper. Parents loved

this because the children were so actively involved.

John Lane

The open-air pool

People may recall the swimming pool at Brockington. A lot of money was raised to build it and I think it was used for some ten to fifteen years — this was quite a good life-span for an open-air pool. Eventually, one winter, it cracked so badly that it could no longer be used, and it was filled in. It is now beneath part of the current playground.

John Lane

two

Growing up

An aerial photograph of Enderby, late 1970s.

Falling off my bike

I remember that when we were still fairly young, about fourteen or fifteen years old, it was a regular occurrence for half-a-dozen of us to get sandwiches, egg sandwiches in particular, and cycle out to Hanging Stone Rocks in the forest. We'd sit there and eat our sandwiches, or whatever we'd got that time, then belt back as fast as we could to be in time for Sunday school at half-past ten. I always remember coming down Blaby Road and one time turning into Co-operation Street a bit too quick and falling off my bike! There was a car that stopped, luckily, and out got Doctor Brown, our local MD. He just said 'do you want to kill yourself?' I said, 'no', so he said 'well, don't do that again'.

Jean Carter

Girls' Training Cadets

It was something to keep us off the streets more than anything. The boys had the army cadets and the air force cadets. We used to meet at Townsend Road School. Mr Swanson and Mrs Harris were over us – Lizzie Harris and her daughter Thora. Mr Swanson used to take us for square-bashing, not exactly like the army, but I suppose more like advanced girl guides. We had to do training for the square-bashing, but nothing to do with weapons. I was about fifteen-and-a-half when war broke out.

Dorothy Williams

Barclays Bank Cottages

Clive's grandma lived in one of the cottages which are now the bank. She'd no back door, and she had to come out of her house and down the entry, where the bank door is now, to get to the toilet and to get water. She'd bring the water in a bucket, and she'd no sink, so all the washing-up water went into the drain outside. The place was lit by a paraffin lamp. When we were courting, we used to go to Charlie Cherry's chippy across the road for a bag of chips, then go to Granny Gillard's to eat them.

Norma Hall

Childhood games

We made a game with the tops off the milk bottles, which were cardboard, and had a hole where you put the straw through. We'd put a marker on the floor, and then skim the top to try to get nearest the marker. We played whip and top and snobs. We were very naughty at times, and used to play knock-door-run.

Jenny Smith

The Nook, 1971. Pam Lawrance lived at No. 28.

'Down the bunny run'

When we were teenagers, we used to go to church on a Sunday night, and then come straight out of there and go down Blaby Road by the mill, to the bunny run to meet boys from Narborough, Littlethorpe, Whetstone and Blaby. They all used to go down there.

Mavis Almond

Safe streets

We were always outside playing, which was ok as there wasn't so much traffic in those days. You could play out in the streets quite safely. I remember once leaving my bike on the recreation ground – it was still there a couple of days later.

Ted Brown

Washday

I think it was better for doing the washing in The Nook than at Narborough Wood Cottages, where we used to live. There, you had to wash on a certain day in the big communal copper. I think my mum had a boiler in The Nook; gas, I suppose.

Pam Lawrance (*née* Preston)

Nature walks

We went on nature walks down the Green Lane, which was nice. As you came out of Bantlam Lane, you went down there, and you could come right round and then up Mill Lane. We'd pick celandines and violets, it was a lovely time. We used to go to places we shouldn't. We'd go down to the quarry in

Seine Lane, either to play or to take a picnic. If any of us had ever fallen in the water there, we'd never have got out because none of us could swim.

Pam Lawrance (*née* Preston)

What to do in the village

I went to the chapel youth club. We used to play table tennis, dance, listen to records, chat, play darts, just meet up really. I used to take sandwiches up there to sell, things like cheese and potted meat. Sometimes, we'd go to Whetstone youth club, or they would come here. Other times, we'd go to the Co-op Hall for a dance. I also went to Carlton Hayes for the dances. My Uncle Ray worked there, so I was able to go with my cousins on Thursday nights to watch pictures there. We sometimes went to the cinema in Leicester, but we never saw the end of the film because we had to leave to catch the last bus.

Christine Bryan

Listening to the radio

Of course, for entertainment there was only the radio, there wasn't any television when I was younger. They used to have Victor Sylvester and his orchestra on, and I remember I used to say to my dad, 'Oh, let's dance, dad,' and he'd let me stand on his shoes while he danced. It wasn't proper dancing because he didn't go dancing himself. I was always allowed to stay up for Bruce Woodcock's fight – those sorts of things used to be on the radio – and there was *Dick Barton*. We had to be home to listen to that at about a quarter-to-seven in the evening. I suppose it was a way of getting us kids to come home because we were allowed to play down at the old breach, at the back of the top chapel.

Joyce Fawell

A boot up the backside

Me and my mates used to go round the lanes in the daytime. We'd go into the Hall grounds, across to the pond, and round by the quarry, but we never did any harm. We'd take a short cut across the chapel cemetery and across the churchyard into Leicester Lane, and then round the estate. Our biggest obstacle there was Jeff Neale, the gamekeeper. He just didn't like us on his estate, and one day, he chased us off across Leicester Lane, and who should be coming up from Braunstone police office but PC Dixon. We scattered into the churchyard, and I got down behind a large gravestone. I knew full well he couldn't see me, but a little old lady was coming back from getting some water, and she shouts, 'Here he is, Mr Dixon'. The next thing I knew was a boot up my backside, and my head going into the wall.

Barry Bryan

The billiard table

One Christmas Eve, my dad asked me if I'd like a billiard table, and, of course, I said yes. We went down to a little sports shop in High Street, and saw one in the window. We decided that was the one we wanted, and went into the shop. My dad said he wanted the billiard table out of the window, and the man in the shop said we couldn't have it. My dad said that if we couldn't have that one, we wouldn't have anything. We had the one in the window!

Arthur Cherry

Playing in the quarry

I spent most of my time as a kid with the Rourkes. We used to go over the fields to Thurlaston. Opposite where we lived down Seine Lane there was a big quarry. In the quarry they had what they called 'Blondins'.

It was a scaffold with a rope that went down into the quarry and brought the stone out. We used to go there quite a lot, and when Harold Rourke went to work there he said, 'Let's go round the quarry and I'll show you where the crushers are. Would you like to see them run?' This was about eight o'clock at night, and it was dark. He switched it on and it just turned over and stopped.

Laurence Lilley

The Co-op Hall

When I was at school, they used to have dancing classes at the Co-op Hall. We used to have Mrs Winterbottom doing Scottish dancing. Oh dear me, I can hear her now saying, 'Point your toes'. That was used for all sorts of fêtes and dances. We had our wedding reception there. They had plays as well. It was very well used by a whole range of people from Enderby. It was just an old wooden building where the Co-op car park is now. It had a wooden floor, which was good for dancing. There was a little kitchen at the side, so they could do functions, parties and things.

Joyce Fawell

Brownies aloft!

Veronica Belton used to run a brownie company in the Red House, in Broad Street. It was on the third floor of the house, in the attic. When you were a little brownie, and used to look out of the window, you seemed a very long way up!

Judith North

Dancing the fairy ring

When I first started with the guides, we used to meet at Danemill School Annexe in Townsend Road. After a while, when Brockington College was built, we moved into the hall down there. My earliest recollection of guiding was when I first started in the Brownies. We used to meet in the Mission Hall in Moores Lane, and I vividly remember we used to dance our fairy ring round the coke stove in the middle of the room. When I was talking about this recently to Chris Thompson (the minister at the mission) he said if you look up at the ceiling, you can still see the vent where the old coke stove went out into the sky.

Claire Timmins

After school

I went out and played with all the children in the street 'cos me husband lived in the same street – whip and top, shuttlecock and battledore. There wasn't much else to play.

Edna Burgess

Losing my torch

When it was dark one night, we were coming home from school. My mum fetched my sister, Rita, and me. My dad had bought me a torch, it had one of those big glasses on it. When we got nearly home, my mother said, 'Turn the torch off, you'll waste the battery', so I did. Just then, something big walked by. It was a bloke with a great big dog the same height as me. It frightened me to death and I dropped the torch. I found it by feeling round, and went to switch it back on but it had broken the bulb. My dad wouldn't buy me another bulb.

Lawrence Lilley

Special Occasions

I can remember one time, I don't recall the year, when Lady Baden-Powell came to Leicester and we had a big rally that we all

Enderby guides and brownies, Salonika Reunion Association parade, 1937.

went to, and, of course, every Remembrance Sunday, we joined in the British Legion parade, the Brownies, the Guides, the Scouts and the Cubs. In wartime, the Home Guard paraded as well. It used to be a very big parade in those days, with the Enderby band leading the way to the church. We started at West Street, marched all the way to the church. There used to be an annual parade of the guides in Leicester that we used to go to. We marched from town round to the cathedral, and then the lord-lieutenant, or someone important like that, would take the salute on the town hall steps. We did a certain amount of drilling in those days, but it's now gone out of the programme. It's more relaxed these days.

Claire Timmins

The fair

Mother was a housewife and we lived in Alexander Avenue, which is where I was born.

She came from Blaby and my dad came from Beggars Lane. His dad was a farmer and there were thirteen in his family. My father was a mental nurse at Carlton Hayes Hospital, which was a huge place. I remember as a child they used to have a fair come round every year. My dad always used to get the job of helping to put the roundabout up. He hated it, because they'd get on you see, the patients, and then wouldn't want to get off. They'd perhaps be sick, and things like that. They also had a cinema at Carlton Hayes that we were allowed to go to on a Friday evening, and they had a wonderful ballroom. When we were older, I used to go to dances there.

Joyce Fawell

Scout camps

In the summer we used to go away for a week's camp. I remember one campsite in Oxfordshire for its outdoor swimming pool – it was covered with a thin layer of green algae! Needless to say, we didn't use it. We used to go to Nottinghamshire and one year there was a drought so we helped the fire brigade fight grass fires. It was very exciting but exhausting for the boys. Another year we went to Yorkshire. We tried to have a day out from each camp we went to, and this particular year we went to Sheffield. We were shown round the headquarters there and I remember being taken upstairs to see one of the windows. When he'd visited there, Baden-Powell had signed his name on the window with a glass-cutter. I guess that by now that pane of glass has been taken out and preserved rather than leaving it in the window as we saw it.

John Lane

The quarry pool

We used to have a bit of a football team at

school with Albert Cox, Ken Knight, Charlie Hinton, Roy Kendrick, all the lads, but we only played the local villages. It wasn't run by the school, just us getting together. We also played down the quarry a lot, although we shouldn't have done. We used to go down to what we called the 'Tips', down Mill Hill, and do a bit of fishing down Blaby Road with a piece of string and a bent pin. It was where the scout hut is now, but then it was about 200 feet deep and filled with water. In the winter, it used to freeze over, and we used to slide on it until we heard it crack – a bit dangerous when you think about it now! When it cracked, we'd scurry back a bit smartish. We'd go down to what we called the 'pancheon' field down Harrolds Lane. It had a big dip in it, and we used to roll down from top to bottom. There was a spinney at the bottom with a little stream running through it, and we used to paddle in it. There were blackberries there too, the hedges would be black with fruit.

Stuart Buzzard

Camping under camouflage

It (Enderby guides) has always been a very active and thriving company with a great variety of activities. It's always been a camping unit and there has been a camp every year for as long as I can remember. Even during the war years Miss Lee was involved with the Women's Land Army, but she used to take us camping. We used to camp up at Enderby Lodge Farm at Lubbesthorpe. We had to camp in camouflage tents under the hedge so that we weren't very visible. We all had to take our rasher of bacon and a little bit of butter and sugar, because in the days of rationing you couldn't just go out to the grocer's and buy all the stuff in, but we still had great fun doing that.

Claire Timmins

Enderby scouts in the new scout hut.

Falling through the ice

One winter, the pond at the back of the old chapel had frozen over, and us kids went down there to play. This lad went and put his foot through the ice and filled his wellington with water. Instead of making him walk home to warm up, we decided to take him home on a sledge. There he sat, shivering and teeth chattering.

We used to take picnics down there. Once, a friend of my mum's, Mary, even brought the kettle and made the tea.

Joyce Fawell

Life in The Nook

Living in The Nook was very, very basic. You hadn't got any light upstairs, you had to take a candle to bed. You shared the toilet with your neighbour, and the toilets were emptied by the council. It wasn't very nice. When they came round, you'd do a runner. We did have

1st Enderby Girl Guides, 1935.

running water there, but it was very basic for my mum to cook with. We'd got the bath in front of the fire, which was very nice and warm, the old tin bath.

Pam Lawrance (*née* Preston)

The bunny run

We used to go down to the bunny run, by the hump-backed bridge past the Foxhunter, on the road to Whetstone. There were loads of us used to go there in the war years. The land used to flood, so we stood on planks down there. There were lots of girls and blokes got together down there, some even got married. There was one lad who could tell jokes all night long. He'd get on a plank, and there'd be twenty or thirty of us saying, 'Come on, Alf, tell us another one'. And he'd be there, telling jokes while the bombers went over. There was never any trouble down there. They were happy times.

Arthur Cherry

Using my time to the full

My life was full of enjoying myself so I didn't sit about. No, I'd sing and do all sorts of things. As I got a bit older, I got to joining little clubs. We played tennis down Blaby Road, where the old pit used to be. There was three hard courts there. In Enderby, everyone knew everyone and we used to do things together in little groups. We did some mischievous things like a bit of scrumping now and again, if there were any gooseberries or anything about, and of course, we never got into any trouble. We'd go to the recreation ground to play. Sometimes, we'd go down to the mill and take a little jam jar with a bit of string round the top, and a net on a stick to do some fishing. Our mothers used to give us a penny, and we'd go to the shop and buy some kali and mix it in a bottle of water so that we had something to drink out there. We'd come back from the stream at dinner-time, then go off again after dinner. Where the cricket field is in Enderby, we'd go past there, then over the Narborough Road, by Enderby House and then you'd be at the mill and the field where the stream was.

Sadie Jayes

Out on the town

After we had played football on Saturdays, we used to go to the working men's club, which was near the cinema. We used to pick up our girlfriends from there and go to the pictures and have a nice evening. On Sunday mornings we used to go down to the 'Reccy' which is opposite the cricket club. We used to go to the Olympia cinema on Narborough Road at night-time, then on to the Saracen's Head, in Market Place. We had to get a bus in Western Boulevard by eleven o'clock, otherwise we had to walk home.

Lenny Fawell

A stage career?

When I left school, I said I wanted to go on the stage. I didn't want to go out to work! But when you think back, there was no way your parents could afford such ideas. I could sing or turn comedienne or anything. If any of the concert party forgot their words, I could always prompt them. They would always say, 'Sadie'll pull them through', and I did.

Sadie Jayes

Scout honours

Pamela and I were invited to one of the royal garden parties to represent scouting. It was a real pleasure to go to Buckingham Palace, along with a few thousand others, but at least we were there, and it will always stand out as a memory. We've been to Windsor Castle for the St George's Day parade too.

John Lane

Playing out with no cars

When the aerial landmines had dropped, we collected the bits of shrapnel and bits of aeroplane glass, like perspex, which we made into rings and things. We played football in the street because there were virtually no cars – they were taken out of use except for the military. We also played whip and top. For the lads in West Street and Stewart Avenue, our playground was the grounds of Carlton Hayes Hospital. We'd climb the trees there. The hospital was built in 1905.

Arnold Young

Youth Club

When I came out of the forces in 1948, I got involved in forming a youth club. Me and Les Wilson set up a club for the kids in the village. We used to meet in Townsend Road school once a week for about two years. There were various activities – we had concerts, film shows, visitors from other youth clubs. Pauline Mellor from Narborough was a member.

B.T.

Doctor Berridge's water

Doctor Berridge used to live up Moore's Lane, and there was a water stop-tap outside his house. When we were kids, we'd turn off his water and run away. When he found out, he'd be down Daniel's Yard, where we lived, saying, 'Where is the little devil?' I always got the blame. We used to play in his field. He had a couple of cows in this field, and we used to build a house with the cut hay. Once, we got a fire going, and it got out of hand, so we ran down to the church. We looked back up Hall Walk and the smoke was puthering out. He never did find out who did that.

Ernie Yeomanson

Wakes Fair

This was the highlight of the year. It was on Mill Lane when I went, but it must have been coming to the village for donkey's years

Cliffe house, Moores Lane, home of Doctor Berridge.

Enderby Wakes Fair, Mill Lane.

because it used to be at the back of the (Plough) pub on Mill Hill. Of course, you hadn't got much money, so you didn't get to go on too many things, but as I got older, it was a good place to meet the boys! We had dressmaking at school, and I made this dress, a sort of pinafore dress, and I thought I was the bees' knees in that.

Joyce Fawell

The concert party

I crammed as much as I could into my teenage years. I played tennis and did ballroom dancing, and I was in the concert parties. There were five boys and five girls from the village and two of the schoolteachers. Enderby had an 'odds and ends' concert party made up of men and women. When they'd performed, we were the junior 'odds and ends'. We'd go to all sorts of places and put concerts on. The school in Townsend Road had a big partition through the middle of the two big rooms, and we pushed that back to make one big room

Sadie Jayes

Street games

We used to play football and cricket in the street. We'd play in Mitchell Road because there were the allotments at the end. Mr Jesson was the local police constable, and if we saw him coming, we'd sit down on the kerb until he'd gone. We played hare and hounds – one team would go and hide, maybe in Alexander Avenue, Mitchell Road, George Street or up the fields round by what's now Sloane Close. The other team would have to go and try to find them. Sometimes, we'd play tin-a-lurky, where one person would have to kick a tin as far as they could, and while one person went to get the tin, the others would hide. Where there were palings in front of the houses, we'd make a tent out of an old sheet or something, and sit in it to have tea. A man called Tony used to come round with his ice cream van in the thirties. The only time we went knocking on doors was when there were fireworks for bonfire night. We'd go round as guys, asking for a farthing or a halfpenny to help us out. We had some good parties for the Coronation or the Jubilee. There would be a row of us in the street, and again the ice cream man would come round.

B.T.

three

Shops and Businesses

A group of ladies from the Congregational church in front of Rose Dobson's shop, Chapel Street, in the 1890s.

Working for the Co-op

I started work in October 1918, six weeks before the Armistice was signed. This was at the Co-op office in Croft. In Enderby we had penny bank on Mondays. We had to do all the books. Fridays we paid the wages – we had to come home for tea, then go back until seven.

When I first started, I got about 12s 6d a week, and when I first started, Harry Biggs was the manager, but he wasn't there very long before Mr Gittings come. Then, of course, when he died my husband was made manager.

There was a grocery shop in John Street, and the one on the Cross, and the butchers round the corner, and the drapery next to it. Finally, they had a shop on the corner of King Street, it was the butchers later on, then they moved the butchers to where it was part of the grocery now. They haven't got a butchers now, it's all pre-packed, you see.

Edna Burgess

The blacksmith

There was Alfred Webster's blacksmith's shop on the top of the hill. I remember how he used to shoe all the quarry horses. Then there was also Billy Lowe's shop. That faced the Plough.

Laurence (Curly) West

Walking the pig

I used to keep a pig in George Street. I'd watch it feed, then it would come round the back of me and put its head on my lap and go to sleep. I'd take it on a rope up High Street to Jayes' butchers to get it slaughtered. He'd ask me if I wanted to watch, but I couldn't – it was like a pet.

Ernie Yeomanson

Jayes butchers

It was Sid Jayes that had the butcher's shop. He had a son who was married, and he (Sid) bought the farm at the back of the shop and put him in it. It didn't work, though. I think it was Joe Hulbert that bought the farm off him. My husband used to go down there for the milk. Hulberts left the farm and came to live next door to us in Alexander Avenue.

Sadie Jayes

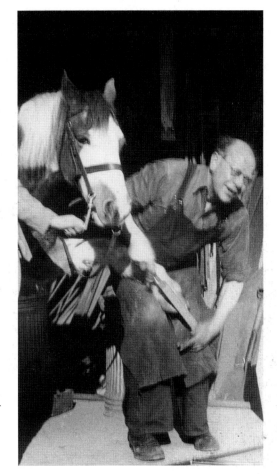

Alfred Webster, blacksmith, shoeing a horse.

A generation of butchers

Father was born on the farm between here and Huncote – Cooks Lodge. Mother had a very chequered career because her people were butchers, and the butcher's shop was at the bottom end of High Street opposite the old school. It's a granite-built house – I suppose that's valuable these days. There's a monument in the schoolyard to Charles Brooke and he lived at Enderby Hall at that time.

My grandfather, it would be, had a butcher's shop in the High Street, and, I don't know if it's still there, there was a double door because most butcher's shops had these so that

you could open the top one to let the air get in. Charles Brooke used to talk to my grandfather quite a lot.

On the Cross in Enderby, where the Conservative Club is now it was, there were a lot of beer shops. I think it was home-brewed beer, and he (Mr Brooke) was a strong teetotaller. He offered to build a new butcher's shop for my grandfather, an ornamental one. It's still there now – if you go up High Street past the Conservative Club on the left, it's where Michael Freer's shop was.

Doris Webster

Freer's butchers shop, High Street.

Feeding the fowl

The main Co-op store was on the Cross. You could get bran there to feed the chickens. I used to go up there for my grandmother to get bran to feed her fowl. If you kept chickens or anything like that during the war, you were entitled to get bran to feed them, but you didn't get any eggs from the shops. The other Co-op grocery shop was called the cake shop, and was on the corner of King Street and Mill Lane. They had cakes on a Saturday morning. There was a shop in John Street where you got your milk and bread checks from, and the butcher's was in Mill Lane, next door to where I lived. I think he was called Dick Bird. The drapery was next to there, where you could get suits, dresses and so on, and then they extended it to sell furniture and electrical goods. Finally, there was the Co-op

Hall where you used to get dances on Saturday nights, parties, and other functions, a well-used place.

Stuart Buzzard

Buying sweets

The shop opposite the Plough, that was my in-laws. The main window was made up of little glass panes, and then at night time they'd bring wooden shutters. It was a grocer's shop and off-licence, and they used to have the bottles of sweets.

D.L.

Village shops

At the end of King Street were the butcher's shop and the greengrocer's. At the top of John

Mill Hill and Conery Lane, 2000. Lowe's shop was on the corner.

Street was a big house with a wooden garage at the side. Butch Jayes used to serve meat out of the garage. A bit further down, where the electric shop is now, was a Co-op shop, and a bit further down, on the other side, was Alf West's sweet shop.

Roy Coulson

Part-time at the Co-op

When we came back from Scotland, there was a job advertised at the Co-op, in the drapery, so I went there just Thursdays, Fridays and Saturdays. I worked there, with Herbert Gilliver, for about two or three years. They had clothes and haberdashery, and at Christmas, there were always the Christmas gifts. There were always queues of people waiting to collect their money from the savings stamps when it was released just before Christmas. There was also the Co-op bank at the back of the shop, and the electrical department. We bought our first colour telly there.

Beryl Seymour

The threepenny-ha'penny club

The threepenny-ha'penny club had been running for a number of years. People used to pay threepence ha'penny, or multiples of that amount, each week for most of the year, and then in November, there would be a payout of what you'd paid in to buy food and gifts for Christmas. It looks as though the Co-op are going to start the dividend again, just like they used to.

Herbert Gilliver

Jack Bradshaw and Mrs Bradshaw in the 1980s.

Co-op drapery with Mr Bates. They used to sell everything there, televisions, lino, garden furniture. Mr Bates used to take me on the train to Manchester to buy goods. One time he took me was when kipper ties were in fashion. I asked him to get some because some of the lads in the village would like them. He wasn't keen but he got some and said it would be on my shoulders if they didn't sell. They all went! They were ever so garish, not at all like what the Co-op usually sold.

Pam Lawrance (*née* Preston)

The sweetie barrow

We used to go down to the spinney, just below where the school (Brockington College) is, and, of course, there was always the old oak tree down Mill Lane. There was a big oak tree with a hollow in it, and on Saturdays, Jack Bradshaw used to come down with a barrow with children's sweets in it. There were aniseed balls, eight for a penny, and things like that. All the children used to gather there, waiting for Jack. It was a big treat.

Mavis Almond

Spence's news

Mr Spence started up selling papers. He started where the paper shop is now, but he did it out of his front room in those days. He used to walk very fast, did Mr Spence. You could hear him coming a mile away because he'd got a hell of a voice on him.

Nigel Cooper

Kipper ties at the Co-op

It was a very close village then. When I first left school, I went to work in C&A in Leicester, but I left there and got a job in the

Bradshaw's shop

To me, Bradshaw's shop was a high-class, old-fashioned grocer's store. I don't recall them actually weighing things out separately, but you could get freshly sliced bacon. They wore white aprons, and used to deliver. You could get everything you needed there, right in the centre of the village. This was in the 1950s.

Sheila Thorpe

Enderby village in the 1960s. Bradshaw's stores is on the right.

The caravan chippie

In Rawson Street there was a small plot of land. A couple bought it, put a caravan on it and started a fish and chip shop. Their fish and chips were beautiful. There was also Cherry's fish and chips in the village. We used to go for a drink on a Saturday night to the ex-servicemen's club, then come down home and get some fish and chips. They'd say, 'We've got some scratchings here', and they'd put a pile in a paper for us. We'd take them home and our dogs loved them – a real Saturday-night treat.

Sadie Jayes

The fish cart

Opposite Cyril Shenton's nursery in Rawson Street was Sid Orton's fish cart. Apparently, it was a horse-drawn cart that would go up to the Plough car park, but I can only remember it stationary, no horse, in a garden in Rawson Street. Behind it was a brick build-ing where Sid used to peel his potatoes. The chips were beautiful, and there were queues everywhere. Sid was always sipping from a bottle of nut-brown ale, but it didn't spoil his chips.

Barry Bryan

Cherry's fish shop

My granddad set up the fish and chip shop in 1878, and he ran it until he retired when I was very small, I could only have been about a year old. My mother and father took it over and that's when I came from Cosby to Enderby. My father kept the chippy until about 1953. I used to help my father do the potatoes, all night peeling them by hand. Me dad had three prices, fish and chips for a penny, for twopence or for threepence. There were always plenty of scratchings. My dad always used to wait up, he'd never close until the last bus from Leicester came along at half-past-eleven. Every night of the week for as

Cherry's fish and chip shop. Arthur Cherry and his sister.

long as I can remember, a group of chaps a bit older than me used to come in for their fish and chips. Some nights, they'd say to my mother, 'Hang on, Lizzie, we're going for some watercress'. My mum'd say, 'Where the hell are you going for watercress?' and they'd say, 'Down the brook, against Joe Hulbert's farm, round the Hardwicke'. Sure enough, they'd come back with armfuls of watercress to eat with their fish and chips.

Arthur Cherry

The smell of the shop

At the bottom of Cornwall Street was Frank Young's shop, and when you went in there, it was like going back in time. There were vegetables outside, and inside there was everything you could think of. You could get anything there, and the smell was beautiful. He always wore an immaculate white coat. At the back of his shop there was a German helmet hanging up.

Barry Bryan

Brookes' Shop

We moved to the Cross, next door to Brookes' shop. My sister and I used to squabble about who took the rent money into next door, because whoever took it got a penny or tuppence back and we thought a lot of that. I think the rent was only about ten shillings (50p) a week. The Brookes family had three children, Ivor, Maureen and Audrey. Brookes' shop was a sort of sweet shop, but when you went in, you had a job to find the sweets. I don't know why, but they had another room at the back that Mr Brookes set up as a hairdresser's. He was a man who was always whistling, whistled everywhere he went, you couldn't miss him.

Lawrence Lilley

Getting a paper round

When I was ten, me and my mate, Jeff Attenborough, were walking down from Jack Bradshaw's towards Mill Lane, when a bloke came out of the cake shop, which was where Forget-Me-Knot is now. They also sold papers, and he was the manager. He asked us if we wanted a paper round, but as he'd only got one round going, it would be first come, first served. I knew Jeff wouldn't be able to get up in time, so I made a special effort, and got the job, seven and threepence a week. I shouldn't have been doing it as I was only ten. We used to take the papers all down Equity Road when it was a mud bath along there. We had to deliver to 'Baconbox Bungalow'. It was a horrible house, made partly of bacon boxes, and some called it Mouse Hall. I also took papers down to Pen Craig in Harrold's Lane. There was no electricity there.

Barry Bryan

The cycle shop

On the corner of Mill Lane and Rawson Street, there used to be a cycle shop, I think it was Tommy Palmer's. He had two sisters, one didn't go out much, but the other did. He used to come out with a jug in his hand at lunchtime and off he'd go, up to the Nag's Head, I think. He'd have a couple there, then bring a jugful back. How he ran that shop, I don't know. The lady that lived there wasn't really well, and she'd open the window in the morning and throw her clothes out. The kids used to laugh at her on their way to school.

Sadie Jayes

Buying your cigarettes

There was one (shop) at the top of Chapel Street, opposite the chapel, and when we were kids, we had, you know, we had a cigarette now and again. You could go in there and buy two cigarettes and a match for tuppence. I used to take mine down to Rourkes' house, down Seine Lane, because they were great friends of mine. I used to spend all my spare time down there. There was Alfie Rourke who was about the same age as me, he became the school caretaker, and his brothers, Arthur and Harold.

Lawrence Lilley

Mobile tradesmen

When I was a young lad in West Street, it was lovely. There was a bloke who used to come round with the milk cart, and I used to help him. The milk would be in churns, and he would ladle it out and take it to people's houses. We used to knock on the doors and ask if they wanted any milk, then we'd pour it out of the jug we had. Tommy Winson would come round with his horse and cart when I was very

small, although he soon went mobile – he got a van or a lorry. He had his store in a little lane opposite my house in West Street. There was also Ken Barlow, who was in competition with Winson for fruit and veg. A bloke called Robert Williams was the baker, and he used to live down the bottom end of West Street. He'd sell bread straight from his van.

Barry Bryan

Not many sweeties

There was a little shop in the front room of one of the houses still standing near the King William pub (in Shortridge Lane). It was run by Mr and Mrs Brookes. I can remember the counter now. It was just like a scrubbed wooden top, and we used to get liquorice sticks from there. I was so young when the war started, I didn't know there were so many sweets and things to be had.

Joyce Fawell

Bloxham Jayes, one of the village milkmen, in King Street.

Co-op bank

You had to go upstairs to the (Co-op) bank. That's where Mr Burgess was in charge. He was secretary to Mr Gittings, and it's where they paid out the 'dividend'. At one time, it came to two and sixpence in the pound. You had checks for the bread and milk, and you had a Co-op number for everything you bought. My mother's number was 348.

Lawrence Lilley

Twopennyworth of chips

The shop we used mostly was on Cross Street. There was a Mr West used to work there with a big white pinny on. There was Bradshaw's shop, and the old chip shop next door. You could get twopennyworth of chips. I was sent there once when my auntie was with us. I can't

The old Co-op building in Cross Street, 1999.

remember now whether it was three two's or two three's, but I said it to myself so many times as I ran along Brook Street that I got it wrong when I got there. Still, you could get twopennyworth of chips and a few free scratchings. They used to have a heap of coal just at the back of a bit of curtain that they used to fire up the chip pan.

Joyce Fawell

A little bit off

You didn't get staff discount when it was Enderby or Wigston Co-op, but you did when it became Leicester Co-op. Even then, you only got discount on dried goods, not on food, but they get discount on everything now. Every Christmas, because I'm a past employee, I am allowed three weeks when I can get a discount on food.

G.C.

The ghost of Enderby chippy

Before my granddad took over Enderby chip shop, it had been a sock shop. The story goes that a new lady started working there, and for some reason something fell on the floor. She turned round to pick it up and asked who knocked it off. The other ladies sat and laughed at her, and told her it was all right, it was only the ghost! Another time, I had an uncle staying with us. I thought I saw a shadow in the room, and he told me it was all right, it wouldn't hurt me. When I asked what wouldn't hurt me, he said the ghost. To this day, my sister and I believe that shop was haunted.

Arthur Cherry

The Co-op dividend

Everybody that joined the Co-op became a member by paying so much – a pound, I think it was – and you had a number. When a customer came to pay for their goods, you would ask their number and you'd write it on a ticket, along with the amount they'd spent. The ticket was in triplicate, and one copy would go up to the office. It would be calculated once a quarter, and a dividend would be paid. I remember the dividend being as much as two and six in the pound, which was quite a lot. Mind you, things didn't cost as much then, so you had to spend quite a bit for a high bill. The dividend was well-liked, but it must have been a terrible job in the office to calculate all those tickets. In those days customers were allowed credit, but you had to watch it because some people would run up quite large amounts of money. I was really glad when credit stopped.

G.C.

THIRTY-FIRST
QUARTERLY REPORT & BALANCE SHEET
OF THE
ENDERBY INDUSTRIAL PROVIDENT SOCIETY,
LIMITED,

Registered No. of Society, 1238.   *Enrolled* 1868.

To the Members,
    The Committee have to report to you the result of another Quarter's transactions. The turnover for the quarter is, Enderby £1074 6s. 9¾d., showing an increase over last quarter of £15 12s. 0½d. Thurlaston Branch, £241 1s. 7d., making a total for the quarter of £1315 8s. 4¾d. The number of members is 248, increase during the quarter, 4. The Trade Profits of the quarter are £131 6s. 7d., which the committee recommend to be divided as follows :- A dividend of 1/9 in the £ on members' purchases, and the usual dividend of 9d. in the £ on non-members' purchases.

GEORGE FREESTONE, President.

The QUARTERLY MEETING will be held in the National School Room, on Tuesday Night, Oct. 24th, at 8 o'clock. Dividends will be paid at the Stores, Enderby on Wednesday Night, Oct. 25th, and at Thurlaston on Thursday, Oct. 26th, commencing each night at half-past Seven o'clock.

Attendance of Committee.

Mr. G. Cliff	9	Mr. C. Young	11	Mr. J. Haines	8
- S. Coulson	12	- G. Freestone	13	- J. Bradshaw	10
- T. Storer	13	- R. Spence	10	- W. Nixon	4

Thurlaston Branch Committee.

Mr. T. Hewins		Mr. W. Pegg		Mr. J. Wardle.

Storekeepers—*Enderby*, Mr. W. Burgess and Miss Rodds.
       „   *Thurlaston Branch*, Mr. W. Riley.

Mr. R. BURGESS, Treasurer.
Mr. E. MARSTON, Secretary.

Enderby Industrial Provident Society, report and balance sheet, 1876.

The first pomegranate in Enderby

Mr Toon's shop sold everything. When the pomegranates came, he was the first man to have them. All the kids who could afford to buy them (we couldn't!) had one.

Lawrence Lilley

Delivery boy

I used to be the delivery boy for the Co-op in John Street in the 1950s. I had a bike with a basket on the front to deliver the groceries. I got 2s 6d a week for that. My pal, David North, was delivery boy for the Cross Street shop. He got about five bob a week because it was a bigger store.

Ray Bingley

'What you got for ten shillings?'

Bacon was about 1s 11d a pound, cheese, you'd get for ten (old) pence a pound, oranges were a penny each, a quarter of sweets was about fourpence and half-a-pound of biscuits would be sixpence. You'd get a lot for ten shillings, but then wages weren't very high, were they? When I first started working in the Co-op, I got twenty-five shillings a week, and it gradually went up until I got about £100 a week when I finished there. We used to get paid in cash. When I was manager, they'd send me a wages slip, and I would have to make all the wages up. You could have the money put straight into the bank if you wanted to. I know some people did.

G.C.

Moving house

I married Herbert Jayes from the village. We lived near one another, started courting and got married. I was born in Rawson Street, and when I got married, I got a semi-detached

Enderby village centre, with the Co-op store built in 1939.

house. Then we bought a house in Cornwall Street, and from there, we moved two or three doors down to a shop. It used to be Young's shop, then another chappie had it, and we bought it from him. It was a double-fronted shop, and we sold hardware – my husband was a carpenter, and he did painting and decorating as well.

Sadie Jayes

The caravan chippy

Well, there were two chip shops in the village. The one I'm talking about was down Rawson Street. It was an old caravan with the fire range up at one end. You'd climb the steps and queue up in the other little bit. They were good chips. The people who worked there

liked a drink, they'd be sweating away cooking the chips and drinking at the same time.

Lenny Fawell

Rationing

I can remember the post-war rationing. The weekly allowance was 2ozs of butter, 4ozs of margarine and 2ozs of lard, which is more like cooking fat, 8ozs of sugar and 4ozs of tea. We all had ration books. We used to have a special offer each week, and you could have one thing or the other. Things just weren't available, were they? There were a couple of kinds of soap powder and soap flakes. Everything had to be weighed up, even the tea. Biscuits weren't in packets, they had to be weighed out of a tin. Bacon you sliced on a machine, which you don't do now because it all comes ready done. Every shop had a bacon machine, which you cleaned down every day. The Thurlaston shop had no heating. You had a coal fire and a bucket of water to wash your hands in. Very primitive, it was. I used to go out there on a moped with things from the Enderby drapery store. People would ask for particular things from the drapery department, and I would take them out with me.

G.C.

Taking the milk round

The milk was all in churns on the milk float, three churns at different heights, and we had a plunger. We also had a big box of eggs. Before you filled the bucket up you always had to stir the milk, because the cream came to the top. You couldn't let all the customers have as much as they liked because it had to go round everyone. There was one lady in Alexander Avenue who'd have no end of milk if you'd let her. You'd have to let her have two or three pints, then say you were sorry she couldn't have any more, or you'd run out before the end of the round. The last customers were always in John Street. They had to have what was left, like. I can remember the very last customer was Mrs Phipps. She had to have what was left.

Nigel Cooper

Co-op bank

There was a bank at the Co-op where the main offices were. They called it the penny bank, because you could put in as little as a penny if you wanted to. I remember a great-aunt of mine used to put a penny a week out of her ten shillings (50p) pension, and when she died, there was quite a large amount saved.

G.C.

Co-op committee, 1940.

Enderby Co-operative Society 'checks', found in a field next to Enderby church.

Treacle Bradshaw

When I was a young lad, I remember going into Bradshaw's shop. We used to call old man Bradshaw 'Treacle'. People asked us why he had that nickname, and we said it was because during the war, when treacle was rationed, he was the only man who could get hold of it.

Barry Bryan

Co-op checks

They used to have milk checks and bread checks. You bought these in the shop and got your dividend on them, then put them out to pay for your milk and bread. I think the roundsmen carried check books with them so that you could get your dividend if you paid cash. The checks were metal at first, but then became plastic.

G.C.

four
Working Life

Young's shoe factory workers, King Street, in the 1890s.

Recruiting the workers

My mum worked in the hosiery, in Tommy Hurst's factory in King Street. She was one of the first to go and work there because, I think, she knew Tommy Hurst from working in Leicester. When he was building the factory up and wanted staff, he'd say to me mam, 'Can you get me a machinist or an overlocker?' Me mam would think who she knew while she was getting the dinner, then she'd go off and get him his workers. My two sisters both worked there in the end, because they didn't have to pay bus fare into Leicester, which was a big thing out of your wages in them days. Yes, it was a good little factory.

Nigel Cooper

Starting with the Co-op

I left school at fourteen and went straight to work at the Co-op factory, in the shoes department. We started as what they called the 'runabout', which was doing the errands and sweeping up. After that you went on various machines. When the war started, we went up into the clicking room and worked on cutting the linings for the shoes. I was a skiver [someone who reduced the thickness of the leather used in shoemaking]. During the war I had to go to Standard Telephones and Cables in Aylestone. They made the components for the radios for submarines. I left there to have my daughter.

Dorothy Williams

Quarry maintenance

My main job at the quarry was maintenance in what they called the wagon shop at Warren Quarry. We did all the woodwork and the repair of the wagons, building the wagons, stairs and the walkways on the gantries. When they were blasting, there was a warning to keep out of the way. Our shop wasn't anywhere near, but if you were working down at the quarry doing any repairs and it was getting near blasting time, you'd say, 'Right, lads, let's clear off.'

We'd start at half-seven in the morning, would have a ten-minute break in the middle of the morning, an hour for lunch, another ten-minute break in the afternoon, and we'd finish at around half-past-five. We got about thirty shillings a week in the late forties. It would be the tradesmen who got the higher wages, the fitters, the blacksmith, the loco-maintenance men, the welding shop, the electricians shop and the wagon shop. It would be only a few pounds.

Jeff Steer

Dad's coal round

Well, me dad's coal yard was against what they called 'the wharf' at Narborough station. There was Jeffcotes and the Co-op in the same yard as well. Ellis's was at the back of them. It were all horses and carts in them days, and the stables for me dad's horses were next to Empire Stone, in Park Road. They used to have three or four horses stabled there, and every night, when they'd finished work, the horses had to be rubbed down, brushed and polished, then given a feed and a bucket of water. Then me dad had to get on his bike and take the horses, two on either side, to the field next to what is now Narborough Reccy. He had to fetch them back again next morn-

Mr Cooper, village coalman, outside Enderby church.

ing. I remember that one of the horses played up once, and put its foot through me dad's bike wheel. Me dad had to have an argument with the firm to get his bike mended, as they said he shouldn't have had his bike there when he'd got four horses. Anyway, when the horses were all harnessed up, they would take them round to the station where the carts were, and load them up with coal. Me dad used to do one day in Cosby and one day in Enderby, and that's how his work went on. Some people would want ten bags at a time, but he'd say, 'You can have two and that's your lot!' In those days, the coal was graded – so there was the mucky slack and the mucky nuts. If the coal was in good lumps and it shone well, then that was good coal, but if it was dull, it was muck and it wouldn't burn well. There used to be no end of arguments about the coal in them days. It was really hard work for the horses to pull the cart up the hill near Woodlands to Enderby from the station when it was loaded up.

Nigel Cooper

Milk rounds

Maurice Hulbert had a farm across the road from the Hardwicke. The farm had a milk round, all round the village. In them days, I used to pal out with Maurice, although he was a bit older than me. I used to go down with him and milk the cows in the morning if I was off school. He had a pony and trap, and we'd take the milk round the village, but in them days, I dread to think how many milkmen there were. There was Mr Spence, who was up again where Next is now, Mr Hutchinson, and Mr Henry across the road from Hulbert's farm. That was Thornhill farm, it's all houses and the school (the Pastures) now. Then there was the Co-op; they had a round as well. A lot of the girls worked for the Co-op in those days, as did Mr Thorpe, Bernard's dad. He had two different jobs; he was either the milkman, or if he wasn't doing that, he had the fruit and vegetable shop in King Street. The Co-op had a small shop in King Street. The dairy was at the back of where the bookie's used to be, and the shop was at the front. It was a paper shop as well.

Nigel Cooper

Co-op shoe factory

I left school at the age of fourteen, and went to try for a job at the Co-op boot and shoe factory in King Street. If you could get into the clicking department, you were lucky, and as it happened, there was a vacancy going there which I applied for, and got. I left school in the month of December, and started work early in the following year as an apprentice clicker. A clicker was the person who cut the uppers and linings for the boots and shoes. I think I got paid nine shillings (forty-five pence) a week, so the wages were poor. That was in 1934.

Frank Humphrey

Clickers

I was a clicker at the Co-op factory in King Street. When I first started, you used to have a pattern. You used to have your skins of leather and the steel patterns, and cut round them by hand. I've still got my clicking knife. We used to make them ourselves. Mine was made from an old hacksaw blade. From there, the work went into the prep room, then into the machine room, and into the lasters. It then went into the finishing room, and finally into the stock room. We used to do all ladies' shoes, no men's. We used to be on our own time, piecework. It wasn't hard work, unless you got patent leather – it was freezing in cold weather, and the steel patterns weren't very warm either. The funny thing was, in the summer, when you could have done with something cooler, you were making bootees for the winter, with sheepskin linings, and the sheepskin was flying all over the place. When I first worked in the factory, I was about sixteen or seventeen. We used to go in at nine o'clock in the morning, and they'd tell you there was no work that day. We often got that until, I think it was the Labour Party brought it in, if you were called in to work, they had to find you two hours' work. Then they brought out the three-quarters wages, if they called you in, they had to pay you three-quarters of your basic pay. That was in the 1930s. The factory used to run departmental cricket matches. The clicking room, lasting room and finishing room all had teams, and we played other factories on a ground in Belvoir Drive. I still get a pension from the factory. I worked there for fifty years.

Roy Coulson

Living near the quarry

Warren Farm, where we were born, came right up to the quarry. At twelve o'clock every

Enderby Warren Quarry, 1986.

day, the siren would go, and we'd know they were going to blast, so we took shelter. I lived on the farm until I was sixteen, and only once did we have any granite fall into the farmyard – but it was a huge piece. On the edge of the quarry lived old Joe Neale, the gamekeeper, he was even nearer than us. The workmen used to start about six in the morning – it was very hard work. You could hear the drills going, then the blasting, and they worked until five o'clock. The quarry at Stoney Stanton was going at the same time, and I used to cycle over with my brother to watch them working. It was a tough life for them. The Enderby quarry workers used to live in little cottages in the village, down Quarry Hill. They've been made into lovely little places now. Gradually, the quarry spread towards the farm. They had to take a lot of soil out to get to the granite underneath, and this was piled up near the farm.

Molly Broomhall and Joyce Turner

Skiving

I was a skiver in the shoe trade. We had to do various widths and depths, and take the extra off with a knife as it went through the machine. If the leather had to be folded, it had to taper down so that the two thicknesses were the same depth. If anything was overlapping you did what was called overlap, and where the seams were at the back, you had to take some off so that they could be machined properly. Sometimes we had to put in back-straps and tongues as well. We were on piece work – and if I earned three pounds then I'd had a good week. When the work we'd done left us, it went to another machine that cemented what had to be folded. There were various little buttons you pressed. One nicked it all, so that it went round the corners flat, and then another pleated it. Herbert's factory was in John Street, and Ward's was in King Street.

Dorothy Williams

The shoe trade after the war

By the time the war ended, I'd seen quite a bit of the world. I'd been to India, Burma, Malaya, and I was finally discharged from Japan. I was there in the army of occupation for six months. By the time I got back home, the Co-op shoe factory had closed as an active production unit in King Street, and had moved to Knighton Fields, so I went there to continue where I'd left off before the war. Things were a bit difficult then. It takes quite a few years to become a skilled clicker and you started off as a fitting cutter. The principle of using a knife and cutting to a pattern was the same for the linings and the outside leather, but the knowledge of the leather wasn't the same. You learned this in the later years of your training, so it usually took six or seven years to become a skilled clicker, which brought you up to the age of about twenty. Well, of course, when I came back from the war, I was old enough to be a clicker, but I hadn't done all the training – the years when I should have been doing the later training, I was away in the war. There were a good many like me, so we set about learning as quickly as possible. No two skins are alike, so you had to learn all about the qualities of leather, and how to cut it and use it to best advantage in the production of shoes. We were doing ladies' shoes at the time, so it was an extremely skilled job. We got back into it eventually.

Frank Humphrey

The bakehouse

My auntie worked at the bakehouse and they wanted some help. My mum said that if I wanted to go she'd look after the baby. It were more for the Christmas rush really, but I was there for about three years. We done all the fancy cakes. They'd got a tart machine. We used to have to weigh the pastry and put it in this big round thing, pull the handle down and it cut the pastry into little oblongs. We used to stand there and put the pastry into little

Old Co-op bakery, Co-operation Street, 2000.

patty tins and it went round, pressed it down and then cut all the waste pastry off. There were sixty on a tray. Then there were the other buns, the cream buns. We had to roll them, the dough was made downstairs but we were upstairs in the confectionery. They didn't cost much in the shops, maybe twopence or something like that. They used to be sold in Enderby.

Dorothy Williams

Lonsdale hosiery

I went to work for the factory opposite what is now Barclays bank in 1950, and we moved down to where Smarties is now in 1955. I started as a runabout and finished as a supervisor. Lots of ladies worked there, and some of them were real characters. We turned out some lovely work, nightwear mostly. Once, when we first moved down to West Street, the ladies kept coming in and noticing a smell. Each one thought it was one of the others, but it turned out to be a dead rat! It was under the floor.

Norma Hall

A near miss!

I went back into the shoe trade after the war, but I was training as a surgical-footwear maker. I wasn't completely happy because, in 1947, my father and I were travelling back and forth on the bus. 1947 was a dreadful winter, and one day we were coming up Blaby Road by the old quarry when the bus skidded. There used to be a little wall near the quarry, which stopped people falling down there. Well, it was only that wall that stopped us going down the quarry! At about the same time, they were advertising for a warehouse manager at the Co-op, and, as I had been doing that sort of work in the army, I applied for it, got it, and that's how I came to work for the Co-op.

Herbert Gilliver

The Lonsdale knitwear factory, on th corner of West Street and Shortridge Lane.

My family

My parents were Iris Spence and George Jayes, and were both born in the village. Mother was born in Conery Lane and her grandfather built two houses in King Street. He lived in one of them, and his brother moved into the other one. They were called Spence, and Grandfather Spence originally came to Enderby to work at the quarry. He used to walk from his home in Coalville to the quarry in top hat and tails to be the foreman at the quarry, and then came to live in the village.

The Jayes family were butchers in the village but my father was a dental mechanic in Leicester. He was the bell boy, and then went into the practice. A lot of people in Enderby had their dentures made or repaired by my father.

My parents bought their house at the end of Broad Street when it was built, and moved in as a newly married couple. I was born there. They built a house in Equity Road when I was fifteen, the one we live in now,

and when we were first married, we bought the house next door to the one I was born in.

Judith North

The milkmen

I remember two milkmen in the village and they always struck me as so different. One had a real old carthorse and a rough old cart with the milk churns on the back. He used to wear a cap, and he had a scruffy beard, an army greatcoat and big boots. The other guy had got a nice-looking horse with a shiny trap behind it. All his milk equipment was bright and shiny, and he was so smart. They were so different.

David North

Working at Holt's

My mum worked for Dunlop's, winding rubber onto a reel. One day, the rubber snapped and really hurt her eye, made a real

The Jayes family from Bromley, Kent, visit Hardwicke Lodge Farm, 1923. Bob Jayes is the driver.

mess of it, so she left there. I walked past Holt Chemicals and saw a notice in the window. They wanted people to work there, so when I got home, I told her, and she went and got the job there. She was doing spreading at the time. They used to have different materials, all cut out, and then they had to spread glue on them and stick a pile of them together. That was a toe puff. After a while, they invented a plastic melted with chemicals, and that was impregnated into a cloth and put onto the shoe. It was dipped in acetone, moulded, and left to dry – it formed a plastic toe-cap. That brought the end of spreading, so they went on to skiving, chamfering the edges of the material so there's no step between the different parts of the shoe.

Alan Smith

a manager to supervise the amalgamation, and to run the new unit. I was shortlisted and got the job, and I did pretty well at it. The depot was at South Wigston at first, then it moved to Western Boulevard in Leicester. A short while before I retired, the general manager at the Co-op said to me, 'Look, you've been a good servant to us over the years. Tell me what you'd like to do for your last few years.' I said I'd like to work in Enderby, so they moved me here to supervise the whole lot. Apparently, they hadn't got a general manager in Enderby at that time, it was just separate departments. I wasn't there very long before I retired, just over twelve months. I was over the electrical, furnishing, clothing and grocery departments.

Herbert Gilliver

Enderby post office

I started to work for the Post Office in 1936, when I left Newarke Girls' School, and I was there until 1947. I remember that pensions were ten shillings (fifty pence) a week when I started, and were paid on a Thursday. That was what you got when you were sixty-five. When you turned seventy, you had to wait until Friday for your money. Family Allowance started in 1946. You got nothing for the first child, but five shillings (twenty-fivepence) for later children, which went up to eight shillings. About this time, something called supplementary started. That was when a person had a pound a week for three months, and an extra twelve and sixpence if it was deemed necessary.

Mavis Almond

From coal to clothing

The coal departments at Enderby, Wigston and Great Glen joined forces, and they wanted

Making nighties

At Lonsdale, the fabric used to come in on a roll. You'd put your pattern on the fabric, and

Herbert Gilliver (wearing chain of office), being made president of the National Co-op Coal Merchants' Federation, 1974.

go round it with a pencil. Then you'd mark another length, and another, and so on. You'd put the pencilled piece on top, then cut them all out together, using shears. Eventually, we got to use electric cutters. When you were a cutter, you had to wear a leather pinny over your apron to stop your clothes getting ruined. We called them belly pads. The fabric then went through all the other processes – machining, overlocking, binding, buttonholing, ironing, folding and packing.

Norma Hall

Moving about with the shoe factory

They decided to re-open the Co-op shoe factory in Enderby again. It was successful up to a point. There were a fair number of clickers about, and quite a lot of ladies for the machining, but as for skilled men doing the soles and making up, there weren't so many of them, and for the job to succeed, there has to be an balance of skills. Therefore they moved us back to Leicester where I worked until I was sixty-four, as a clicker until the last ten years, when they made me floor manager. The Enderby factory closed in about 1950. Eventually, the building was split into several smaller units, and let out. The council moved into the part that had been the Co-op offices.

Frank Humphrey

Explosion at Holt's!

When I left school, I worked for Jones & Shipman, but I felt I wasn't getting anywhere, so I went to Holt's, where my mother worked. I was impregnating the material. There was a big machine, a big drum with paddles inside, and you used to put in acetone and methanol, then tip in a quantity of plastic, put the lid on and let it revolve for about two hours. It came out as a liquid, in which the cloth was soaked,

and made into toecaps for shoes. The plastic we used came from old spectacles, the sheets that were left after the frames had been cut out. We also used old celluloid film.

I was working the late shift, from three o'clock until eleven. We'd had a delivery of acetone and a delivery of celluloid that day, twenty tons of celluloid. That was what caused so much of the flames, it all burned, all of it. An hour before the explosion, Holt Chemicals had been signed over to Vik Supplies Limited. It was 2 October 1972. We were running the machine and soaking the cloth. There was just a loud bang and all the ceiling came in, big lumps of brickwork fell through the glass roof, it just all came straight through. It was the distillation plant that exploded. After we'd soaked the cloth with the chemicals and plastic, it was washed to get rid of the chemicals, and then the washing water was pumped through the distillation

Shoe components factory explosion, 1972. The view outside the factory...

plant to recover the chemicals. It was the distillation plant that overheated, and there was a build-up of chemicals in the brick tower. It somehow ignited and just blew the tower apart, and that's what came through the roof. I dived under one of those big twenty-five gallon drums, and a big section of brickwork come down on top of it, with me underneath. I broke three ribs, punctured a lung, broke three rings on my spine and had various burns on my back. There was a lot of steam used in the process, and the steam pipe broke, that's what burned me. I was in intensive care for ten days, and about the same time on the ward. There were only two of us on that night shift, the other employees all worked the day shift. There were twenty-five women and five men working there during the day. Part of a wall was blown out, and the debris covered the machines where the women worked. Luckily, they'd all gone home, there's no

telling what would have happened if the explosion had been a bit earlier. The canteen was right next to the distillation plant, and that had a glass roof as well.

I recovered and went back to work. The chemical side of the business had stopped. They bought in cloth that was already impregnated with the chemicals and plastic from somewhere else. I think most of the people in Enderby didn't want chemicals back in the centre of the village. Vik had another plant in Stafford, and after the explosion, they did all the production in Stafford, and just brought the material here to be cut up on the presses, skived, and sent out.

Alan Smith

...and inside the factory.

Co-op tea girl

After I left school, I worked in the Co-op offices. I was in the check office for a start – everybody started there – and I was also a tea girl, until the next one came along. We used to have to make the tea and answer the telephone. We were upstairs in the little check office, sorting checks and adding them up for the dividend, and those sorts of jobs. The checks were little pieces of paper that showed your Co-op number and what you had spent. These were added up over a period of six months, then the dividend could be worked out, and we had a dividend day to pay it out. We used to have a full day in Enderby, a half day in Narborough, an hour or so in Thurlaston and Braunstone to pay out. I was in the check office for about two years, then I went into the main office. There, I did the wages, the tax returns, the mortgages and the loans and shares. It was an interesting job and we were all friends, Mary Cox, Joyce Bailey and me. Mr Burgess was our boss, and there was a young man called Gerald Wagstaff. His sister was in the back office. She dealt with the milkmen who cashed up there. Gerald eventually took over her job, and later became manager of the Tamworth branch. Herbert Gilliver was in the warehouse, and George Clarke was one of the managers. I remember him being at the Crossroads branch.

Eileen Briers

The old white fiver

My dad was a wagoner – he used to look after the shire horses, and he did numerous other jobs on the farm as well. My mum worked in the fields at the farm. She used to put me under the hedge in a pram when I was a baby while she did her work. She told me once that she went to cut a field of mangels, and Mr Kirkwood gave her her pay. When she opened it up, it was a white piece of paper. She asked him what it was, and he told her it was her pay. She'd never seen a white five-pound note before. It was a lot of money in them days for my mum, but she had cut the whole field of mangels. She went into Leicester and bought us lots of things, and filled the pantry up as much as she could, but never bought anything for herself, of course. My dad loved the horses. When they were foaling, he'd often stay up with them all night.

Pam Lawrance (*née* Preston)

Making clothes

I worked at Lonsdale for about twelve months, cutting fabric. It was a friendly, family place to work. The fabric came in big rolls, and you cut it to a pattern to make nightwear. Sometimes it was cotton, sometimes nylon. It would be bundled into big bins, and then taken out for the overlockers and machinists. After that, I did outwork for a time, and then I went to Hurst's in King Street part-time. I used to sew press studs on to fasten dresses, skirts and

trousers. At one time, we made some very nice garments for Marks and Spencers. We got paid by the dozen, piece work, so if you didn't work hard, you didn't earn much. It was up to you. I did enjoy being there, we had such fun.

Christine Bryan

Football or footwear?

My father worked as a machinist at the Co-op boot and shoe factory in King Street, and my mother was simply a housewife. During the war, my father was moved to the main factory at Knighton Fields Road, and, of course, he had to travel to get there. In those days, he was quite a good sportsman. He had a trial with the old Leicester Fosse and was accepted on to the team, but in the end he decided to stay with the Co-op. He had just been given a new machine to work, one of the first to come out, called a 'pullover', and he decided to stick with that rather than be a goalkeeper for a few years with Leicester Fosse. We lived at the corner of Brook Street and Cross Street. Eventually, we moved to the house next to the Institute, nearly opposite, where we stayed until my parents died. Fran and I lived with them until we moved down here (to John Street) in 1947.

Herbert Gilliver

Jobs for my mum

When we moved to The Nook, mum worked in one of the factories. She was also working on the tip, sorting the rubbish, down at the Hardwicke. I don't think she thought much of that, sorting the rags and so on. She left there and went on a milk round. I think she enjoyed that, although it was hard work, seven days a week. She used to deliver down to Narborough Road. She had an electric float. We used to have to charge up the accumula-

West Street in the 1930s.

tors in the garage in Brook Street. The dairy was in King Street, where the bookies was. They had to load their own crates, but she got an extra pint of milk.

Pam Lawrance (née Preston)

The violet cart

The violet cart used to come round to empty the pan lavvies. Our pan lavvie when I was a child in West Street is still there now. As you walk up Equity Road, the building is still there, like a little house in the garden of number forty-nine. I don't know why it was called the violet cart. The cart used to come up – the same guys who emptied the lavvies would come round another day on the roller shuttered dustcart. They took the rubbish down to the tip, which was down near Elkes's bakery at the bottom end of Green Lane. That bakery became Marston radiators.

Barry Bryan

Changing jobs

I wanted to work with my dad in the Enderby Co-op garage and be a motor mechanic, but no, he got me a job in the shoes under Mr Smith. He was the man in charge there and lived down Blaby Road. I went into the clicking room. I was doing the tags for the backs of shoes, the bits that join the two pieces at the back. After that, I went on to cutting the insides of ladies' shoes, the linings. They had an extra piece built on to the end of the factory – it's now the Civic Centre – and that became the clicking room. All the chaps went down there, and during the war, one by one, they kept going to fight, and were replaced by women. I left there and got a job at Reid and Sigrist at Braunstone Aerodrome. In the shoes I was on eightpence (less than 3p) an hour, but at Reid and Sigrist I was on sixpence an hour. I had to bike six miles there and six miles back, but you got a small bonus if you worked hard.

Laurence Lilley

Working in the new factory

When I left school, I went to be a hairdresser at the Co-op shop on Mill Lane, but I left there to work at Lonsdale hosiery factory. They made underwear, nightwear and jumpers. It was a purpose-built factory. The business had started off somewhere nearly opposite Bradshaw's shop, in Cross Street, at the back in an upstairs room, but as it got bigger, they built a new factory. I think you earned about two pounds ten shillings (£2.50) then.

Joyce Fawell

Delivering the milk

During the war we had about three bombs jettisoned, one of which landed on the lodge to Enderby Hall in Leicester Lane. Of the other two, one landed in the churchyard, and the other in the field next to it. There were also some aerial landmines which landed above Tom Webster's dutch barn in Copt Oak Road. Tom was a local milkmen, and I delivered milk for him until 1945. The milk was delivered in a pail at that time and Tom used to measure the amount out, usually one or two pints. The horse knew the round and stopped at every house, including the Nag's Head, where Tom would disappear for about fifteen minutes. In 1945, milk had to be pasteurised, and Tom finished then.

Arnold Young

Family work

My mother was a maid at the vicarage. My grandfather was verger at the church and my great-grandfather was verger for sixty years. In the church, there's a plaque with his name on it. Grandfather worked down at the quarry. He was a knocker-up. They used to blast the stone, then he'd have to go with a hammer and break it up into smaller pieces and load it on to wagons, and that was taken away to the crushers. My father was a baker in the bakery, which later became the fireplace workshop. He left the Enderby bakery and went to work in the one at Whetstone. Of course, in the early days, there were no delivery vans, it was all done by horse and cart. I remember, Mr Spence used to bring the bread round with his horse and cart. Bread was twopence three farthings (1p) for a small loaf, and fourpence ha'penny (2p) for a large loaf, and you'd get thirteen cakes to the dozen.

G.C.

Blasting

When they used to blast the granite at Mill Hill Quarry, I was at the corner shop. Well, it would open your ears sometimes with the blast. You had to be indoors at a certain time, in the lunch hour more or less, which used to be 12 until 1 in those days. I think the Warren Quarry was opened at a later date because there were bluebell woods down there. That was the last one to be filled in.

Doris Webster

A quarry village

Enderby had always been a working-class village. It had developed really through the quarries. The limited company started in about 1860. You'd got probably about 300 men working there. My mother's father, Thomas Lowe, worked at the quarry all his life and lived on Mill Hill. He was a kerb dresser. They made granite kerb setts. In later years, it was mainly chippings that were crushed there, and they were transported by rail.

Arnold Young

Above: *Workers outside Marston's knitwear factory, Rawson Street, in the early 1930s.*

Left: *An advert for products from Enderby Quarry, 1919.*

The new Danemill school

Trevor, my husband, applied for the job of caretaker at the new Danemill school and he got it ahead of twenty other applicants. The school was just being built, so he had to do his training at Brockington College. A lot of the staff for Danemill school came down from the church school. There was Mr West, Mrs Lees, Miss Thomas, and Mr Palin – we went by surnames because Mr Jephson, the head-master, wouldn't allow any first names to be used. It was different with the new head. Fred Bates did a lot for the school. He made bird boxes for the aviary and made a lot of our notice boards. He was a governor for quite a few years.

Pam Lawrance (*née* Preston)

Quarry railway

The railway line from Narborough to the quarry was extended across what was later Stewart Avenue. Stewart Avenue wasn't built then, in 1905. The line was extended from the brickworks to the hospital, and I think they used the bricks that were made there. Red Bank Brickworks was where the playing fields are now. Stewart Avenue was named after one of the doctors. It joined the end of West Street, which had been built in the 1880s.

Arnold Young

Mother and father at work

Mother and father were both Enderby people. Father was Bill Brooks. He worked a lot

Dan Burgess's knitwear factory, built in the 1880s.

during the early years in the boot and shoe and hosiery trades. There was a little hosiery shop that went between Rawson Street and John Street, I think it was Marston's. The premises are still there now. He left there and went to work in the old factory in King Street, the boot and shoe factory that was. Then he joined Enderby Co-op and worked on the maintenance with Mr Lighthorne and various other people, doing repairs on the shops. They were based in Brook Street, where the old garage was, where they kept the milk floats and charged them up overnight. He also worked in the dairy, which was at the bottom of King Street behind what was the bookies.

Mother worked in the hosiery trade, at Dan Burgess's at the end of King Street. She was a counter hand, which meant she used to pair socks and put the little transfers on them with a hot iron. Then she worked at home for a time, doing the same job, and Dan Burgess used to bring the work round to the out-

workers. I always remember when I was at the junior school in Townsend Road. – when I came out of school at the end of the day, I'd go down to the big, black shed to see my mother. Old Dan's father used to live in the house at the back of the factory – it's called Fernleigh. I used to go there and he'd give me pocketfuls of apples. He had an orchard at the back of the house and I remember how he used to keep the apples in one of the out-buildings on racks.

Derek Brooks

Working at Danemill

I saw the job advertised for work in the office at Danemill School, and thought I'd love that, so I applied for it. Mr Burgess had retired from the Co-op, but he gave me a reference, as did Mrs Wigfull. I'd done some office work for her in the past. Mr Timmins and Mr Jephson interviewed me, and I stayed there until I retired, and very happy I was. I didn't escape dealing with money, though!

Eileen Briers

Starting at the quarry

I started at Mill Hill quarry in June 1938. I started in the fitting shop with my dad. My first job was learning what all the machinery was in there. The first real job I did there was starting filing things and getting used to all the files and hacksaws, and, after a week or so, they put me on a drilling machine. From the drilling machine, I started to learn how to operate a lathe, and then on to the planing machine. We used to repair parts for the crushing plant. Our job was maintenance or breakdowns, including the quarry pump and the air compressors, and also helping the loco-fitter to re-tube the locos.

Laurence (Curly) West

Co-op bakery

The Co-op had its own bakehouse where they baked the bread, and they had five delivery vans for taking the bread to the different villages. On VE day, I was still at school, but by VJ day, I was at work. I think we had two days' holiday then. I worked on the bread round with a lady called Nellie Darby. There were a lot of women working the milk and bread rounds because the men were still in the forces. For a start, I used to deliver the bread with Nellie just round Enderby. We'd do the top of the village one day, and the bottom of the village the next, so you only had your bread delivered every two days. The other rounds used to go to Braunstone, finishing off at Braunstone Lane, Leicester Forest East, Thurlaston, Huncote, Narborough, Croft, Broughton Astley, Cosby and Littlethorpe. The bakers used to do a night shift starting at nine or ten o'clock, and they baked right through to about half-past seven or eight in the morning. The last lot would be coming off when we were loading the vans up in the morning. We'd go out and deliver so much bread, then come back at dinnertime and the bread would be ready for the next round. The vans for Enderby and Narborough were electric, but those that went farther afield were petrol. When I started, the bread cost fourpence ha'penny for a large loaf, and cakes were about five for a shilling (5p). The bread used to keep for quite a long while because they put a lot of fat in it, longer than it does now. They steam-baked it in coke ovens, not electric, it made a big difference.

Stuart Buzzard

Blasting at the quarry

They used to put a series of holes around the quarry face and drill down at 200 feet deep. ICI used to deliver (explosives) every four or

Marston's knitwear factory, early 1930s.

five weeks. They used to charge up the drill-holes, and the day they were going to blast, they would blow the quarry horn, three times for all to get clear, and twice when they'd finished blasting. They'd bring down twenty to thirty tons at each blasting. Then they used to wonder why there was a lot of vibration in Enderby! The material was taken away by rail down to Narborough sidings. It was all ballast for the railways all over the country. The tar plant started at four in the morning so that the lorries could deliver down south ready for work to start at half-past-seven. There were only two men besides me in the fitting shop, the loco-fitter and my dad, Leslie, who was the fitter-turner. It was very dusty all along Mill Hill when the quarry was working, very hard work for the housewives to keep the houses clean. There was Alfred Webster's blacksmith's shop on the top of the hill. He used to shoe all the quarry horses. Then there was Billy Lowe's shop facing the Plough.

Laurence (Curly) West

Cleaning the hard way

For a start, Trevor couldn't have a cleaner, he had to do it himself until the second phase of the building was complete. I used to go in to help him, and we had to put sand on the floor and then sweep it up. It was a demon! We had to do that in every room, even the hall. When we did the 'Big Clean', everything had to be moved, and the hall floor had to be stripped and polished. Trevor was very proud of his hall floor. When we first opened up, Mr Jephson nearly had a fit because people at that time had got high heels, stilettos, and they made marks on the floor. He banned them all.

Pam Lawrence (*née* Preston)

Uncle Harry

I remember I had an uncle called Harry Brooks who lived in Enderby and worked for the old quarry down Mill Hill on the left-hand side. He used to repair wagons, he was a carpenter. I remember going down there with my dad to see Uncle Harry in the workshops, repairing the old wagons that used to pull the stone up out of the hole in the Warren up to the crushers.

Derek Brooks

Perks for the Co-op employees

Every year, the Co-op employees had a buffet or dinner in the Co-op Hall. They invited their wives, husbands and children. There was a couple came along every year to entertain, one was a comedian, the other played the piano. During the summer, they had a day trip out, three or four coachloads, and we took the day off school. They had a hockey team that played on the cricket field. I think they were called Enderby ladies. My auntie used to play for them, and my grandma would take me down to watch when I was six or seven.

B.T.

From Mill Hill to the Warren

I joined the paratroops in 1942 and I got demobbed in 1947, and returned to Enderby quarry, but it was no longer in Mill Hill, it was down the Warren. The new fitting shop was down the Warren. First, it was the same kind of work, but then a different kind when they built a new crushing plant, more up to date. In 1956, it was all remote control. The crushing capacity was three to four thousand tons a week until the quarry was exhausted in 1977. That's when the quarry closed down and they went to Buddon Wood, near Mountsorrel. The granite was used for roads and ready-mix plants and various building sites. In the winter, when there wasn't much work, they carried on stockpiling for the spring.

It was very dirty on breakdowns. Sometimes we used to work all day and then all night until we'd finally finished the job. When they were actually working, there was a lot of dust about.

Blacksmith's shop workers, Enderby quarry, 1915.

Fitting shop workers, Mill Hill Quarry, 1919-20.

In the first instance, there were no dust masks, but in later years – after 1956 – we were issued with dust masks and tin hats, but a lot of people wouldn't use them because they made them sweat so much in the crushing plant.

Laurence (Curly) West

The Co-op in Enderby

Enderby Co-op employed a lot of people in the village. There was the shoe factory in King Street, they sounded a siren about seven o'clock in the morning, again at lunchtime, and again at the end of the working day. The main grocery store was up on the Cross, and the offices were up there too. There were some garages at the back where they kept some of the milk floats.

Stuart Buzzard

Early vandals at Danemill

I remember once when the children filled all the keyholes with something. We couldn't lock the doors that night. We always had Alsatians. When the kids got onto the roof, Trevor would take the dogs down. They wouldn't dare come down! Even so, we had twenty-six happy years there.

Pam Lawrance (*née* Preston)

The end of the quarry

When I left the quarry, various scrap merchants came in and took it all down to use as scrap. The main crusher was delivered to another quarry. Leicestershire County Council started to fill the big hole in. The pump was working twenty-four hours a day to keep the water down, but when the quarry was three-quarters full, the water found its own level.

Laurence (Curly) West

Derek Brooks' father, fifth from left.

Mobile fruit and veg

My father worked for the Co-op, firstly in the bakery, then on the bread round, and then finally on the greengrocery. He used to take the greengrocery on a horse and cart in all sorts of weather in the thirties and forties until, eventually, he went into the shop where the bookies was. Sometimes, I used to go with him to the early morning market in Rutland Street.

B.T.

five
Worship

St John Baptist church, Enderby.

Aldeby church

Once a year, St John's church, the old church at Aldeby, used to have a service in the field. We'd all troop down there, and a harmonium would be stood in the field. We'd sing hymns round that.

Molly Broomhall and Joyce Turner

Playing the organ

It was through the annual Nightlarks concert that Canon Hibbert asked me one day if I would like to play the church organ, as the current organist was looking to retire. I talked it over with the family, and decided to give it my best shot. Canon Hibbert said he would get the organist at the cathedral to take me under his wing. That was in 1939. I told Canon Hibbert that it looked like there was going to be a war, and that there wasn't much point in my learning to play if I was going to be called up, but when it looked like I'd be stationed in Dover, I decided to approach the vicar there about learning to play. He told me he thought the borough organist would be pleased to help, and gave me the use of his church organ to practise. They'd closed most of the organs down in Dover, and the borough organist was made superintendent of the mortuary. And so I was taught to play the organ by the mortuary superintendent! I was asked to play for one of the chapels there every third Sunday, and that helped me quite a bit. When I came back to Enderby, I had a couple of years under Frederick Holt, organist at St Philip's church, Evington. They were looking for an organist in Enderby in 1947, and I got the job – and I'm still here! After Canon

Enderby parish church choir in the 1930s.

Hibbert, the next minister was Geoffrey Gill. We got on very well for many, many years.

One of the main changes over the years has been the size of the congregation. When I first started playing, the church was nearly full, people sat in the same seats every week. We had really good services at Christmas, and at Easter we did Stainer's Crucifixion or part of the Messiah.

The organ has not been extended, but it has been repaired just once, a long time ago. In point of fact, it badly needs another overhaul now.

Herbert Gilliver

Joining the choir

We came to Enderby in 1963, and were introduced to St John Baptist church by Eva Fox.

She knocked on our door one night, before the roads were made up. It was a horrible night, and everywhere was very muddy. She said that the vicar had sent her. I went with her to the Women's Fellowship, and then we started going to the church. I'm quite sure that our old vicar in Alsager had notified Geoffrey Gill that we were coming to the village and would be two likely customers for the church. That was our introduction to church life. There were about four men and eight ladies at that time in the choir when we joined. At Easter time, the choir sang 'Olivet to Calvary' one year, and the next we'd do Stainer's Crucifixion on the evening of Good Friday. This had been the pattern for about twenty-five years or so. It was not only our choir, but the choirs from the other churches in the village, and soloists from elsewhere.

The choir did concerts every Christmas, and at other times of the year down at Brockington College. There was also a choir dinner once a year. When our children were small, we used to take them to the morning family service taken by Alan and Marjorie Joyce, with help from John Lane. That was always a very busy service, and the evening service also saw a lot more people attending than nowadays.

Beryl Seymour

Getting my Bible

I went to the chapel – the Methodist – but when I met my husband he was a big noise up at the Congregational chapel, and he used to keep all the minutes and go to all the meetings and that. I stopped going to the Methodist. I stopped going just before I should have received my Bible. They gave you your Bible when you were sixteen. I left just before, and I thought they can't grumble at me because I'm leaving before they have to pay for this. But Ralph Langton stopped me in the street one day, and he says, 'I've got your Bible for you'. We had concerts in the chapel, in the schoolroom, and we had little plays. George Jayes was there, and he was a comic. We had a jolly good time. I joined the choir and we used to have choir outings. I enjoyed singing then, but I can't sing now!

D.L.

Building the Methodist church

In 1849, there was the present Sunday school building, then Providence chapel was built by virtue of many dear folk, including my grandfather, Alfred Carter, who gave money to make this happen. It was obviously very well used, and the time came that we needed some more space. In their wisdom, the present church,

which has just had its 116th anniversary, was built. Now, we come down two steps from the old Sunday school, which is now the church hall, and we are in our little church. About twelve years ago, we had a bill for £80,000! This wasn't 'Let's spend some money', we had to have this work done. We had wet rot, dry rot, beetles, everything. So everything, but everything, had to go, including the beautiful old pine reading desk and the pulpit and the organ. We had to dig it all out, so we looked a bit like a mini Coventry Cathedral after the blitz. It was dug out, and then we had to do everything we could to try to get the money, and we made it. We said we'd have to get £80,000 in five years, and we made that, and more, in four-and-a-half. Then, three years ago, we felt that we needed more rooms at the back for a youth club and church work. We set on a builder from Nottingham, I think, to set out a plan for us, and we had two new rooms built on the back, toilets, including disabled facilities, and complete refurbishment. That cost us over £130,000, and again, with a few bequests, donations and grants, we made the money well within the time we'd set. I'm proud to belong to this church.

Jean Carter

Congregational chapel

To be honest, my father was very old-fashioned. We were kept on the farm, we weren't allowed to go into the village, except to go to the Congregational chapel at the top of the village. My brother used to go to the Cosy cinema.

Molly Broomhall and Joyce Turner

Chapel anniversaries

I belonged to the bottom chapel when I was a little girl, and I was christened there. We had anniversaries every year. As I remember, you had your best dress, and you practised new hymns and songs. Your aunts and uncles came from all over, and you paraded round the village, then sat on the platform in the chapel. The older you got, the higher up the platform you sat, so when you got to the top, you thought you were the bees' knees. Then, of course, you progressed to the choir and sat in the choir stalls.

Jenny Smith

The Methodist sandwich

In the old days, we used to call our service the 'Methodist sandwich'. This consisted of a hymn, a prayer, a hymn, a reading, a hymn, the sermon, then another hymn. It sort of fluctuates nowadays because some of our younger preachers, thank God, don't want the 'Methodist sandwich', they'd rather have something more 'à la carte'. It's more flexible now, and that's helped by the newer seating arrangements.

Jean Carter

Starting at Sunday school

I first went to the Methodist church with one of my aunts who lived here, the youngest of the girls. She was a Sunday school teacher, and when I was four-and-a-half, Auntie Em took me to the church and I was in the Sunday school. You might ask is there much difference between Sunday school then and now. Certainly, apart from the teaching and the Bible study, there was. I worked my way, as it were, through Sunday school, being a teacher and then superintendent for many years. We used to have Sunday school anniversaries in those days, sadly not now, like a lot of other churches.

Jean Carter

Chapel life

It was a wonderful life at the chapel, very friendly. We used to have 'anniversaries' for the children. The chapel would be packed with people, chairs even had to be brought in, and there were still people standing in the aisles.

Father was a life deacon, mother was really Church of England, but she gave so much time to the chapel as well – that's how she was brought up, to give time where it was needed. She was one of eleven, and was brought up on a farm at Gaddesby. She was a marvellous cook. She was so involved with village life, Women's Institute, baby welfare. She helped

An anniversary at the Congregational church.

Enderby Methodist church, Cross Street, first built in 1849.

to start the baby welfare service and she started the local Women's Institute with Mrs Smith, the chemist's wife. They gave a lot of time to organising fêtes and dances, and concerts for the Leicester Royal Infirmary - any good cause.

Molly Broomhall and Joyce Turner

Sunday school

My father was the choirmaster and church secretary. He was the superintendent at the Sunday school and Mum was the teacher. So I always remember going to church three times on a Sunday, morning, afternoon and evening, right from being a little girl. It was part of our lives, the church was. When I was fifteen, I went to a youth conference, and that was when I committed myself to the Lord. I've been a member there ever since.

Judith North

United Reform church

Well, I guess I was born into the church. I was baptised there, and I grew up through the church. My mother made sure I went to Sunday school, and when I was in my late teens or early twenties, I was involved in helping to run the church. I was secretary for thirty-five or six years. Originally, the people who founded the church met, as I understand, in a barn in Beggars Lane, back in the early nineteenth century. They would have been dissenters from the parish church who founded what would have been the Independent chapel in 1822, and then as the years went on, they would have joined the Congregational Union. Eventually, in 1972, the Congregational church and the Presbyterian church joined to form the United Reform church. The original chapel is now what we use for our Sunday school,

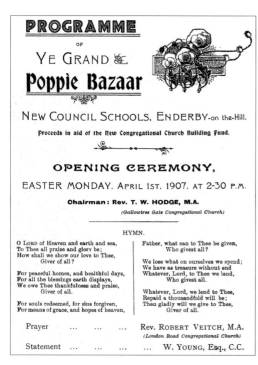

A programme advertising the Poppie Bazaar at the New Council Schools, Enderby-on-the-Hill, 1907.

Enderby United Reform church, Chapel Street, 1999.

and was built at the same time as the manse, where the minister lives. The chapel and the manse were then enlarged in 1847, and they carried on meeting there until the building we have today was built in 1910.

David North

The churches in the village

The Enderby Independent chapel, which was later the Congregational church, is now called the United Reform church, and is in Chapel Street. Several churches joined together. It was built in 1822, mainly by farmers and farm labourers. The original meeting place had been on Beggars Lane. At that time, most of the vicars were absentee vicars. I think one was a hunting vicar who lived in the north of England. He had the tithes from about five churches for his income, and then he would put in a curate to run the churches and pay him a lot less. So for about 100 years, there wasn't a proper vicar. In 1868, St John Baptist was rebuilt and things got back on to a normal footing. I think the only original bit left of that church is the tower.. The Drummond family moved from Yorkshire to be the local squires, and they financed the rebuilding of the parish church. My mother was a member of the parish church, my father went to the Congregational church, and after they got married, my mother joined my father.

Arnold Young

Family Service

The family service at St John Baptist was started by the Reverend Gill and Marjorie Joyce in the mid-sixties. It didn't actually replace the Sunday School because both went

The opening of the new Congregational church, Monday 25 April 1910.

The old independent chapel, built 1822, enlarged 1860.

on at the same time. It tried to bring families with young children into the church. I wasn't involved for the first five years, but I became involved in the early seventies and led the service for quite a few years after that. I always had the support of the incumbent of the time who would give his blessing to what we were doing, and he was usually there to take some part in the service. Our service has now developed into perhaps the main worship service of the day, and the numbers have grown. The form of the service has evolved over the years – things shouldn't stand still. In the early days, children stayed in the service throughout, but now there are special classes for the children. They leave the service about a third of the way through to go to teaching classes, then rejoin for the end of it. Different styles, different needs…

For many years we were about thirty or so for a family service. I don't remember there being fewer than that. I would think the service is at its largest now with upwards of sixty in church most Sundays. It has been very rewarding for me to be involved with the family service, to see the children grow into adulthood and take their lives to all parts of the country.

John Lane

Sunday school treats

We had Sunday school treats at the Methodist church, but we didn't go far. If we went to Bradgate Park that was quite a day out, you know. We'd hire a bus, and we had a great big clothes basket into which we'd put the sandwiches, the lemonade and the cakes, and off we'd go and have a really, really good time. Just the simple pleasures of life, but it was lovely. Prior to that, down where Coleridge Drive is now, of course they were all farm fields and we used to go down there, where the old Enderby Town used to play. Mr

Deacon, who was a member of the Methodist church, was a farmer, and he used to let us have this field so that we could have races and generally enjoy ourselves with loads of pop and sandwiches and stuff like that. Again, the simple pleasures of life. Now, we have to have outings to Cadbury World and the like, on buses. That is one of the big differences between then and now, although the teaching of the Bible is just as important now as it was then.

Jean Carter

Ringing the church bells

My uncle taught me how to ring the bells. I think I must have been about thirteen or fourteen then. After we'd done our practice on a Monday night, we'd climb through the bells and onto the top of the tower, and sit round up there, ringing hand bells, for another hour. That was every week.

Herbert Gilliver

Enderby church bells, recast in 1928 from the 1868 originals.

John Wesley comes to Enderby

Another thing I remember, and it's not too far back, was when we at the Methodist church celebrated our centenary, and our minister, Doug Brewer, dressed up as John Wesley. We all dressed up in old-fashioned shawls and clothes, and we had old-fashioned teas and concerts. Going back to John Wesley, Doug Brewer looked really nice, with his tri-corn hat, and he came on horseback, and we were there to welcome him. The only thing was, the horse wouldn't stop at the church, he went on to the pub. He'd been trained well! I think the minister had to get off and walk back. We had some wonderful times in our church with the old members and the old ministers. We invariably invite them back. Only last month, we had our anniversary, and we had back the Reverend Arthur Spencer, who was with us some years ago, and now lives in Mansfield.

Jean Carter

In the choir

When I was at Townsend Road school, Mrs Harris came round one morning and said she wanted me to join the choir. I told her that I was only seven, but she said that didn't matter. She went and saw my dad, and that's how I ended up in Enderby church choir. Bob West used to take me home after the service. I stayed in the choir until my voice broke, then I went bell-ringing until I joined the services. I'm still a member of the church today.

Arthur Cherry

Douglas Brewer as John Wesley. Enderby Methodist church centenary celebration, 1987.

Singing in the chapel

In the chapel we used to have galleries and we used to sit in these seats right up to the roof. You were really with it if you got to the top row. You used to sing a lot, of course, with the church and the church choir. As I said, I was superintendent for many years, and in those days, we had about sixty or seventy in the Sunday school, including about twenty-five or so in the primary department. It was wonderful, and we had some wonderful times.

Jean Carter

Activities in the United Reform church

We have a Women's Guild, which meets every other Tuesday. We have Pilots and Deckhands, which are children's groups and meet mid-week. There is a craft group who make things to sell to raise money for the church, and a quilters group who meet in the church schoolroom. Over the years, various people have used the rooms, even for body-building, and I think Enderby band used to practise there at one stage. The old chapel is used mainly for midweek activities. We also have Sunday lunches once a month – the older folk really appreciate having a meal together, and it's good fellowship for them.

David North

Flexible services

While we have a suggested order of service, which is five hymns, prayers, readings and a sermon, we are very flexible. In actual fact, every other Sunday we have a visiting preacher, a lay preacher or a minister from somewhere else. Some will bring guitars and play, we've had music groups and the music is not always traditional hymns. We have some hymns and choruses as well. Our minister himself plays the guitar and often sings to us. So we have something for all age groups. It's important to try to cater for everyone.

David North

six

Wartime

Enderby ARP outside the vicarage. Canon Hibbert is on the right-hand side, back row, Arthur Capers is on the left-hand side, front row and Mr Jackson, headmaster, is on the left-hand side, back row.

Wartime evacuees

War was declared on 3 September, my mother's birthday. We were at home, getting Sunday lunch, and the siren went off. I was nine. Life didn't change much in the village. By the time I was twelve or thirteen, we were getting a lot of evacuees. One girl I was at school with, her father was on HMS *Hood*, and he went down with it. Another girl in the same class as me, her father was on a troopship going to Africa when it was hit, and he was killed. We had my cousins who lived in Romford, and when the flying bombs started, my aunt sent them here. The youngest stayed with us, the next one stayed with my Uncle Sam in West Street, and the oldest went to stay with her dad's brother.

Eileen Briers

Holiday postponed

I was eight when the war broke out, and we had to cancel our family holiday to Skegness because the government told the population not to travel anywhere.

Stuart Buzzard

Gas masks from the factory

My mother always worked in the hosiery trade, either working at home or for Burgesses or Hursts. My sister tells me of the time she collected my gas mask for me. Hursts agreed to distribute the gas masks in the village, and my sister went and got a Mickey Mouse one for me because I was so small.

Jenny Smith

Call-up

You were kept informed as to when conscription affected you. I wanted to get into the air force, so just before compulsory conscription, I volunteered as an air gunner to go into flying, and when I was called-up, I was sent to Devizes, in Wiltshire. For a start, we had a gunnery course, and we achieved what was known as a gunner – this involved both air and ground work. Then they sent us to learn to be a wireless operator, but my education was too low for that, so I had to forget that idea. At that time, I was stationed at Topcliffe, in Yorkshire. The planes from that airbase were mainly bombers, and manned by the Canadian Air Force, so we saw a lot of activity with the planes going off to do their bombing across the continent. What was important to me was that some of them came back, and if they landed back there, often the tail gunner wasn't alive. We helped many a time to get them out of the planes, all shot up. This was the position they were asking us to volunteer for, but not being that brave, we declined. Air gunners in those days were all volunteers – they must have been mad.

Frank Humphrey

Senior Aircraftman Frank Humphrey, RAF regiment, aged twenty-one.

On duty in Enderby

I remember at school that they put breeze blocks at all the entrances at the beginning of the war. My father had been in the Navy in the First World War. He was too old to fight in the Second World War, so he joined the special police, and was on duty every other night. I don't think there was very much to do in Enderby. I remember him saying that the only crime was the theft of some tomatoes from a greenhouse.

Arnold Young

Guiding in wartime

During wartime we (the guides) learned the Morse code, and we collected newspapers and rose-hips, which were in great demand for making the rose-hip syrup for the youngsters. I remember there was a wooden building on the corner of Cross Street and Broad Street called the Gadget, and we stored the newspapers there and sorted them. We were awarded wartime service badges when we had put in a certain number of hours on different projects. We used to knit balaclava helmets as well. In those days, you didn't go out as much because of the blackout, so you took up these indoor activities to pass the winter evenings.

Claire Timmins

Bombs over Leicester Lane

I was in the fire service, and when the siren went we had to go up to the Dog and Gun. They had a room at the back. The siren was on top of Carlton Hayes Hospital, and when it went off all the inmates had to put their gas masks on.

There was a bomb dropped in Enderby you know. It hit the gatehouse for the Hall in Leicester Lane, and they (the Germans) dropped this stick of bombs. We'd got a dance at the Co-operative Hall that night, the fire service, and we heard this plane droning over. Of course the fire service had to go out, putting the incendiary bombs out at the bottom of Leicester Lane. We knew the next day they'd dropped this stick of bombs on the house and continued down Blaby Road. So Saturday, Blaby Road was closed. They did say there was a light on at Enderby Hall but I don't know if that was right or not.

Edna Burgess

Edna Burgess celebrated her 100th birthday in 2004.

Coping in the blackout

The blackout was a bit of a nuisance. You had a job to find your way about. You had to look upwards to the silhouettes of the buildings to find your way. Coming home for dinner one day, I found that the iron railings had gone from some of the houses. The council had taken them for salvage. You painted the entry between the houses white to help you find your way round.

Stuart Buzzard

Airships

We got to know somehow that the airships were going to come over, and when we were in school, we heard this humming noise coming. We all wanted to get outside and I think we all went without permission, all the kids, out into the playground. We saw it coming over and we opened the gate and followed it from over the school to Blaby Road. Then we watched it go right over to Aylestone. It was very low, you could wave to the people in it. I think it was the R101.

Laurence Lilley

Corn for the chickens

In the winter there were no street lights because of the lighting restrictions during the war, so you didn't go out much in the dark. In summer you could be out until eleven o'clock because two hours were added on to allow the farmers to get the corn in. I remember going gleaning – of course they didn't have combine harvesters then – so there was always a certain amount not gathered in, and people went to gather their own bit of corn. My grandmother, who lived on Mill Hill, kept hens, and we would gather the corn and bring it home for them. We did go with the school and Miss Moore had quite a lot of

A parade along Blaby Road, fund-raising for the First World War.

hens. I think she expected us to give all the corn to her at the end of the day, but I always managed to keep some for my grandmother.

Arnold Young

The shelter

My dad made a thing in the garden, a shelter, but we didn't go down there very often because it filled up with water and it was cold. If the siren went, they used to put us children under the table in the corner of the room, and they used to sleep in front of the fire on the rug. I remember my dad once bringing my brother downstairs, he was fast asleep and all floppy. I remember best when the war finished because of the celebrations.

Joyce Fawell

Jobs for the girls and boys

When we were in the top class, when the sirens went, the girls had to go to the babies' class (the first-year children), and sit with them until the 'all clear' sounded. The boys'

job was to climb on to the roof of the school, so that, if any incendiary bombs landed on it, they could throw them back into the playground, where they could be put out with sandbags or water.

Stuart Buzzard

Wartime as a child

If the siren went, you went underneath your desk, well, you got your gas mask first, but that was the only protection you had. We felt very scared. When the bombs dropped in Leicester Lane, we went under the stairs, because that was the only place for us to go at home, in the pantry. Once, we stayed in there until my dad fetched us out.

Pam Lawrance (*née* Preston)

Digging for victory

I went up to the big school, and finished up in Arthur Capers' class. We used to go spud-picking a lot because the war was still on. We'd get paid sixpence an hour (2½ pence). We got paid at the end of the week, about five shillings or seven and sixpence, which was a lot of money in those days. I gave mine to my mum. We didn't get any for ourselves, I'm afraid. We always had plenty on the table. We used to have rabbits as pets, and then we'd eat them. There wasn't a lot of meat about, but we always had food. There was plenty of bread. If you wanted anything extra to eat, you had another piece of bread. My dad had an allotment, and grew our own potatoes and greens. The potatoes would last from the back end of the year, when we dug them up, through to when the new ones came. The allotment was down Mill Lane, the Oddfellows' land. We had to get our seed potatoes from the cricket pavilion. They'd let us know when everything was in, potatoes,

Above: *Fundraising for the First World War.*

Opposite: *Local Defence Volunteers, later the Home Guard, 1940.*

peas and other seeds, then we'd go down to collect them.

Stuart Buzzard

Bombs

Of course, there were the bombs that were dropped over Enderby, on Leicester Lane. I think it was a Friday night because there was a dance on in the village. I know we had a day off school because there was an unexploded bomb in the cemetery. People said there was another one in the quarry in Blaby Road, but it was never found.

Eileen Briers

Grandparents in the war

My grandparents were Horace and Maud Jacques. They lived at the bottom of Holyoake Street. My grandfather was boss of Enderby Transport during the war, and he thought he would be in a reserved occupation because it was important to keep things moving around, but he was called up and went into the RAF, and was sent out to the Middle East in about 1942-3. My mother tells me they remember the bombing in Enderby, in Leicester Lane, and they also remember seeing the fires of Coventry. Where they lived in Holyoake Street looked out west and, of course, there was no Wimpey estate to block the view, so from their first floor window they would have seen the glow of the fires.

Mark Postlethwaite

Wartime safety

We had no air-raid shelters in Enderby, so we all had to do the best we could at home

during the raids. My mother made a bed for us in the pantry under the stairs. She put a mattress on the stone thrall. My sister and I didn't go to bed upstairs. Instead we always slept in the pantry, and I knew when it was bad because my mother would get under the table. The next-door neighbour came round to our house too, because most of the men-folk were away and we had to look after one another. We were fortunate in the village because we kept chickens, so we'd always got eggs, and we had fruit trees and grew our own vegetables. We never saw a banana or an orange though.

Jenny Smith

The bombing of Leicester Lane

My grandma and granddad lived at the Lodge to Enderby Hall, down Leicester Lane. Their house was bombed in November 1940, but they both survived. My grandma lived to be about ninety and my granddad survived another two years. The first bomb landed on the Co-op field, at the corner of Blaby Road and Green Lane (Kirk Lane now), but that one didn't explode. One landed next to the cemetery and another went off in grandma's back yard. It shook the house down. The roof came down intact – I went to see it the next day. My grandma was thrown under the table, and a beam came down on my grandfather's head. A man named Mr Williams from High Street helped them, as did Arthur Capers, who was in the civil defence. They were taken to the Infirmary. I should have been on duty that night, but I'd gone to a 'do' at the Co-op Hall. We heard the bombs fall, but didn't know where they were.

Clive Hall

Early recycling

Also in the Folly was the Biggs family, Emily Biggs and the others. They had a lot to do with Enderby band. Emily Biggs and her sisters, and Mrs Neale, Walter Neale's mam, they all sorted the paper and cardboard out, and pressed it into big bales which were sent away every so often, because, of course, it was wartime.

Nigel Cooper

A child in the war

I used to go to my aunt's in West Street every Saturday to help her. I'd serve in the shop in the mornings, then we'd shut the shop in the afternoon and go round to the Hardwicke, to Ashmore's farm. Milly, Mrs Ashmore, was my aunt's friend, and we went there for tea. Later on in the 1940s my dad's youngest brother was killed in Africa. I suppose when you're a child, the war didn't affect you so much. It got so that you didn't get up. I mean, when it first started, we'd get up and be under the table. Mum used to make a bed under there, and all the neighbours would come in and sit under there all night. Dad would have to get up and go to work. He was in the Home Guard.

Eileen Briers

'Look, duck and vanish'

During the war years, I joined the LDV, the Local Defence Volunteers, or the 'look, duck and vanish' brigade. I was with them until I joined the RAF in 1941. All sorts of things happened during those days. On a Sunday morning, we used to go up the quarry, rifle shooting down the bottom of the hole at things for training. We were on guard three or four nights a week from about six in the evening until six the next morning. We used to guard the farm up next to the park, it was Mr Turner's at the time. One night, a friend

who was with us decided to sit in a wheel-barrow that leant against the wall. When it was time to finish in the morning, we could hardly move him, he was so stiff and cold. On our way home, we'd catch rabbits in the park, and we'd pick wild mushrooms. I dread to think what would have happened if we'd come across any Germans because we had only one rifle between us, and if we had five bullets we were lucky. We did get more eventually, and some uniforms, but it took a while.

Major Pope was in charge of our unit, and Bob West, one of the schoolmasters, was one of the officers. Then there were sixty or seventy of us in the Home Guard at that time. We used to sleep at the Institute on beds – there were about eight of us. Then we'd go out in the dark, but there was always someone on guard against the door. Once, they dropped a bomb in Leicester Lane that hit Gillard's gatehouse. We were on duty that night, and helped get the injured to hospital.

Arthur Cherry

Coventry ablaze

I remember when they bombed Coventry. Dad got me up and took me to the top of Seine Lane. As we looked across, we could see Coventry burning. I'll never forget that.

Eileen Briers

Hobnailed football boots

It was in the forties, before I went in the navy. When we were at school during the war, we didn't get any sport – you just went to school to learn the basics. I played for Enderby Town Juniors for a start. We used to change at the New Inn and then we played down the Strawberry Gardens. We'd got a field down there. The first team used to play on what's now Coleridge Drive. We played a team out

Ullesthorpe way. They had one of the farmers' fields – the cattle grazed on it during the week, so there were cow pats all over the pitch. Their team used to play in hobnailed boots as people couldn't afford football boots, so the boots they went to work in, they'd play football in!

Jeff Steer

Half-an-hour for a pint

We used to play near the King Bill, all the kids who lived near there, that is, because we had a lot of evacuees from London. They used to put them in what we called the centre. That was part of the school next to the King William, where you used to go if you had school dinners. It was a proper brick building and it had a proper playground. The woodwork shop was at the back, where Mr Insley taught. He married Miss Hall from the school, and they lived in Enderby. In Shortridge Lane, there was Mrs Brookes' shop, which looked straight down Federation Street. It was only a sweet shop, but you couldn't get many sweets then because of rationing. The shop on the corner, which is now the doctor's surgery, was Antill's during the war. Mr Antill and his wife kept that, and Dan Burgess had a little factory on the corner of King Street in them days. Then you had the Co-op factory, the shoe factory. A lot of people worked there. Everybody used to set their watches by the hooter there, at twenty-five-past-seven, half-past-seven, half-past-twelve, and finally at five o'clock. Mr and Mrs Cherry kept the King William, and Billy Heale, father-in-law of Roy Coulson, served there. They used to put a notice in the window to say when they were open – they'd often not open until nine-thirty, and close again at ten o'clock. At about nine o'clock, they'd all be standing in the street waiting for opening time, because the pubs had to ration their beer.

Nigel Cooper

Congregational church men's fund-raising effort for the First World War.

Building the prefabs

I remember the German PoWs building the bases for the prefabs in Mitchell Road. We used to watch them, and in their spare time, they made toys for the local kids. One thing they made was like a ping-pong bat with four chickens, with strings and a bob weight. The chickens used to peck in sequence.

Ray Bingley

Ex-servicemen's club

The club we used was where the old cinema used to be, and my mother-in-law was stewardess there for many years. She was Florence Jayes, George's wife. We did a lot of concerts there, and my husband eventually became entertainments secretary there. It was a lovely place. The soldiers used to come up there, and they'd get up and sing and entertain us all. My husband used to sing as well. They'd have fancy-dress parties and dances. It was great in those days. It went from there to the big club in George Street.

Sadie Jayes

Ration cards

We had ration cards, of course. You had to make do and mend really. My in-laws used to keep the shop opposite the Plough, and my uncle had Bradshaw's Stores, and then my sister was down West Street. You'd only get a little bit of ration and you didn't know where to take it with three shops in the village with your relatives in!

D.L.

Rationing

You had your coupons and you could only have so much. I used to go to a shop in King Street for my sweets. Then there was Antill's on the corner of King Street, where the doctor's is now. My mum used to do a bit of jiggery-pokery with things, she used to swap things, with my dad still being on the farm. He used to bring us fresh vegetables from there, and milk. We didn't go without, really.

Pam Lawrance (*née* Preston)

Wartime sweets

We were brought up in the war on meagre rations. We had a little bit of butter, very little bacon, some cheese, what they called spam and dried egg powder. They tried to get us to have an allotment, or to dig up our gardens and plant vegetables. We used to go mushrooming in the mornings and get chased off by the farmer. Meat was on ration, and clothes and sweets. There were so many little shops in the village that we used to wander round to see what quota of sweets and chocolate we could get. Of course, sometimes we'd go off to Leicester and get in the queues to get what we could. I remember the sweets. There were marzipan teacakes, liquorice torpedoes, aniseed balls, dolly mixtures, Pontefract cakes, sherbets and pear drops. Then we had these lemon things, a bit of liquorice to dip into some powder, sherbet dips. There was Cadbury's chocolate, Dairy Milk and Fruit and Nut.

B.T.

Feeding the family

My father and my grandfather, they had allotments down past Brockington College, and so we had all fresh vegetables and things. My grandfather kept fowl, and my uncle at the top of the street kept rabbits. I used to take the flowers to various people in Enderby and I collected the money, and I took them eggs on a Sunday to help my uncle. We didn't suffer too badly. I think there was a bit of black market in our area.

Mary Cox

Entertainment

You made your own entertainment. There might have been the 'tanner hop' round at the Co-op Hall once a week, that's opposite the old bakehouse, where the Co-op car park is now. A bomb was dropped about a couple of hundred yards from where I lived. There were two high explosives which demolished the house. Mr and Mrs Gillard were trapped inside but I understand the blast blew them under the table, which saved their lives. Two other bombs dropped, one was just outside the cemetery going down Blaby Road way, and the other was just inside Kirk Lane. Neither of these exploded. We went right round to the cricket field the next day when they were exploding them. We always thought they were after the Lockheed factory, that's where Jones and Shipman was on Narborough Road. Perhaps they saw a light in the Gillards' house and thought that was it.

Jeff Steer

Smoke bombs

During the war, we made what we called 'smoke bombs'. We got either cocoa tins or syrup tins and made holes in the top and bottom so there would be an air hole through. We then put rags in them, put a piece of wire through for a handle, set the rags smouldering, and then, by running along, the air passed through the top and base of the tin and made a smoke screen. We all had catapults and went birds' nesting, which you're not supposed to do now, and fishing at the Narborough Brook, as well as playing football and cricket.

Arnold Young

Sirens at the pictures

If the sirens sounded while you were in the (Cosy) cinema, they would get up on the stage and tell you. The only people to move out would be those in the Home Guard, ARP wardens, firemen and such like. When I was there with my pals, we didn't take it that seriously. We used to take a carrot to eat during the films, as sweets were rationed.

Stuart Buzzard

COUNTY A.R.P. Officer's Report

Since my last report which was dated 31st October, enemy activity in the county has been considerable.

Incendiary bombs have fallen at Narborough, Enderby, Sharnford, Sapcote, Osbaston, Swinford, Desford, Wellsborough, Congerstone, Oadby, Great Glen, Sheepy Magna, Allexton, and Sutton-in-the-Elms. A serious fire was caused at Stackley House, Great Glen; apart from this there was no appreciable damage.

High-explosive bombs and parachute mines to the number of more than 200 have been dropped, and considerable material damage has been done, notably at Melton Mowbray and Kirby Muxloe, but the damage cannot be regarded as excessive when the total weight of explosives used is taken into account. Viewed in the same light, casualties have not been heavy although six persons were killed.

High-explosive bombs were dropped at Welham, Enderby, Melton Mowbray (where machine-gunning also occurred) Birstall, Walcote, Cotesbach, Bottesford, Sharnford, Wellsborough, Cadeby, Twycross, Higham, Stretton, Swinford, Ashby Parva, Croft, Newbold Verdon, Kirby Muxloe, Sheepy Magna, Sileby, Kibworth, North Kilworth,

Saddington, Wymondhan, Bittesby, Willesley, Narborough, Shepshed, Lubenham, Edmondthorpe, Leicester Forest West, Quorn, Rolleston, Barwell, Thurlaston, Sewstern, Packington, and Asfordby.

The mobile canteens have been in operation in Leicester City, Coventry and Birmingham, also at Melton Mowbray, Kirby Muxloe and Asfordby and have proved of the utmost value.

The WRVS has already made its worth apparent in raid welfare and no praise can be too high for the promptness and organisation which provided shelter and meals for some 300 people following the Kirby Muxloe raid.

Speaking generally, the bombing which has taken place has, in my opinion, in no way affected the determination of the public to hold on, but it is useless to deny that the nervousness of already nervous people has been increased especially in the city and its immediate surroundings, and as a result of this, large numbers are trekking into the country districts at nightfall, usually by car, to find shelter where they may. Should this redistribution of the night population continue, and night bombing ensue, a strain will be thrown on the services located in rural areas far beyond anything anticipated or so far experienced, and some movement of parties at night over considerable distances will be inevitable.

W.T. DOWELL.
County A.R.P. Officer
28 November, 1940.

Soldiers in the village

During the war, there was the Co-op Hall where they had dances, and that's where I learned to dance. There would be a dance every Saturday night, and sometimes there would be one during the week as well. There were soldiers based at the bottom of Leicester Lane, and they would often come up to the dances too. The soldiers were there to start with, then it was displaced persons who came along. There were Polish people there. In fact, there were also soldiers billeted in the village, and my grandmother had one. Then she had a displaced person as a lodger. You had to have them if you had any spare room and it was the same with evacuees. When the war was on, they sent evacuees to Enderby, and my grandmother had to have some of those as well. Before the war, there was a scheme where they would send children from London to Enderby for a holiday, to get them out into the country. You could go out at night – we used to play out in the dark, hare and hounds, – it was quite safe.

B.T.

End of the war

We had a very big bonfire in the middle of the street and we were all dancing round it. Then this lady asked me if I would I like this fancy dress she'd got. It was all net and beautiful, I'd never seen anything like it. She told me not to go too near the fire because of the sparks.

Joyce Fawell

seven
Sport

Enderby Town Football Club, Champions 1929/1930.

Enderby Cricket Club, 1911.

The bowls club

I first started and my father was very good with quite a lot of the lady members. He taught them quite a lot. I joined up with a lady who had been bowling for a few years and took part in competitions and was rising up to Leicestershire standard. We won quite a few things at the time. The county held a number of records at the time, but not all of them. She was an excellent bowler, her name was Sue Clarke. Considering ours was a small club, there were some excellent players. Lots of times we joined forces in the pairs, and sometimes we got through to Leicestershire. One time, we got to play at Wimbledon. We were runners-up in the All-England Fours.

Mary Cox

The opening of the new clubhouse for Enderby Bowls Club by Mr Salt, 1937.

Playing cricket

I started playing cricket in 1928 as soon as I left school. It was on the same ground as it is now. You weren't allowed to practise on the proper pitch on Monday nights, you had to get the practice wickets out and save the match wickets for Saturday. If you didn't turn up to get them ready, you was lucky if you got picked.

We played against Wigston, Blaby, Shilton, Narborough, Barwell, Hinckley Amateurs, Hinckley Town and Ratby. Well, the first match I played with Enderby as a lad in short trousers, was at Barlestone, where there were no boundaries, you had to run every run. That day I went in to bat with a fellow I worked with, Harry Barlow, and he got eighty-eight. At the end of his innings, he was so tired we had to undress him. I didn't get that many runs, but I stayed in with him.

Roy Coulson

Not much of a sportsman

I can't say I achieved much in sport. We entered the school sports, and I had some success in the long jump. I don't know when it was, but I can call to mind being selected for the long jump in the mid-Leicestershire sports, which in that particular year were held in Enderby.

Frank Humphrey

Tennis in Enderby

As a youngster in the early thirties, I knew of three lots of tennis courts in the Enderby area. There were two grass courts owned and run by Dan Burgess, the older Dan Burgess. Close by, was what was then the Enderby Town football pitches on Hulbert's Farm. There were also two grass courts owned by the Enderby Congregational church down in Chaucer Street, in what we called Tankey Land. The proper Enderby Tennis Club was on Blaby Road, and what a tragedy it was for us that these courts are now a house and garden. Two courts there were built by intending members in the late twenties/early thirties. The third court, fronting onto Blaby Road, was again built by members several years later.

Ted Brown

Enderby Town Football Club

My grandfather was very involved with the football club in Enderby right from when he was very young, in fact, he was a goalkeeper when he joined them. He went on to become chairman. It was his inspiration and dynamism that managed to get the clubhouse built, the facilities built and the social club, that was all part of the same building programme. He had the idea of bringing sport to the village, that's why there were so many pitches there. I think that at one point there were seven or eight pitches on that site in George Street, so it was a terrific facility. I remember as a child that he was behind the tote, and he would drive us round while he did the tote run. This involved him going to various pubs in the locality, to Croft, Earl Shilton and so on. It always seemed as if he had to have 'one for the road' at each pub he collected from. God knows what state he was in when he got back! I remember when he got back though – he still had huge bags of money with him – in all, it was a very successful scheme.

Mark Postlethwaite

Marking the pitch out

I first started in 1950 with Enderby Town. I played for the Enderby team and our pitch was at Strawberry Gardens. We had to change at the New Inn and walk down. Through the season my granddad and myself used to mark the pitch out. When I was sixteen years old, I played for the first team, and from then it developed, and I had a good career with Enderby Town.

Lenny Fawell

Cricket cup

My father was a keen cricketer. He played for Enderby and was a fast bowler during the 1925-1927 period, in Division One of the

Enderby Town Football Club, late 1970s.

South Leicestershire league. Enderby was the first team to win the cup three years in a row between 1925 and 1927.

Arnold Young

Enderby Athletic Football Team

We played down Strawberry Gardens, in Seine Lane. My brother played, and I remember how sometimes I got a game. The first season, they were top of the league, but, of course, Enderby Town poached most of the good players. Enderby Town used to play down Mill Lane, opposite the cricket ground, long before they went to George Street. We used to train in the skittle alley behind the King William, by doing skipping and boxing. We only went one more season, as we lost all of our players.

Ernie Yeomanson

Changes at the bowls club

When I first started bowling, it was all very regimented. One had to wear a certain hat, a certain skirt, so many inches from the ground, white, of course, all white for club matches. Now they've relaxed it a bit and you can wear grey for some smaller practices. You had to have a certain hat, and the hatband of

Enderby Athletic Football Club.

your own club, your own design hat band, but you did have to conform. Well, it's more relaxed now, and you can wear trousers, and you don't have to wear a hat. This is a bit unusual for me because I think ladies look lovely in their hats, but, of course, you have to go with the flow.

Mary Cox

Public tennis courts

The public courts in Mill Lane, along with the bowling green, were built as part of the Coronation celebrations in 1937. En Tout Cas built both. They were good courts, but slower than the ones on Blaby Road. During the war, the club courts on Blaby Road gradually deteriorated while the ones in Mill Lane were well maintained and well used. After the war, along with other players, we founded a new club on the recreation ground courts. Norman Hunt was secretary and I was treasurer.

Ted Brown

My dad's hundred

My dad was the first man to get a century for Enderby. I can remember playing once and batting with Billy Poyner. I'd made a decent score and Billy said to me 'Go on, get a hundred, then I would have the pleasure of batting with both you and your dad getting to a hundred'.

Roy Coulson

Enderby Town in the FA Cup

My grandfather died when I was eight or nine. Enderby Town Football Club had been his life, and this had a great influence on me and my brothers. We followed the club, and watched every match, home and away. We used to travel on the team bus, all over the

From left to right: Captain Drummond, Horace Jacques, Ted Warry, Mr Drummond, Jack Grewcock (speaking), - ?-, Arthur Capers at the old football ground, 4 September 1957.

country. When we first started watching them, they were in the East Midlands Regional League, and then they were promoted to the Southern League. The first game was against Bedworth. I remember the only time they got into the FA Cup, first round proper, was a great day. Unfortunately, they were drawn against AC Leamington rather than a league side, but we still went with them on the bus. That day, Aston Villa didn't have a game, and a lot of the Villa hooligans decided to come to that match. Me and my brother went for a walk before the match, just in the local area, and we passed some of them. They were walking towards the ground and they said, 'Oh, it's great, they've brought a couple of coaches, so there should be a good fight today.' Luckily, we didn't have our scarves on, and we were only kids, so it wasn't too bad. This must have been in the seventies, when football hooliganism was taking off. I saw one of our supporters'

coaches arrive and there were some of these Villa fans waiting for them. As soon as our supporters got off the coach, a fight broke out, and it spread right across the road. So there was a bit of aggro before the game, and when the game started, we lost 6-1. It was just terrible, and what's more in the second half, there was a pitch invasion. The great thing though was Alf Headley, who was connected with the club. He stormed right out onto the pitch and led them all off. Then on the coach going home, we listened to the five o'clock sports report, and heard Enderby Town mentioned for the first time, but it was for a 6-1 defeat unfortunately.

Mark Postlethwaite

Whirlwind

Just before the war, we had a new cricket pavilion. Shortly afterwards, there was a whirlwind and it moved the pavilion about two inches. It also took the top off a tree just inside the reccy.

Roy Coulson

Two good men

The cricket field belonged to Captain Drummond and the rent was about five shillings (25p) a week. He did a lot for the club, as did Arthur Capers. He was a great man down there.

Lenny Fawell

Playing the Villa

I played for the cricket team. We finished football in April and started cricket, then finished cricket in August and started football. It worked out just right. I played on Joe Hulbert's field after Strawberry Gardens, then we went across to Enderby Town Football Club. They played Aston Villa who won the

FA Cup, and Stanley Matthews opened the ground. I was away in the army then.

Lenny Fawell

Stan Matthews comes to town

I played for Enderby Town when Horace Jacques and Ken Moore were there. I can remember Stan Matthews coming to the village because he came to the Co-op there. I can also recall when Aston Villa won the FA Cup, and they brought it with them one night when they came to play in Enderby. At that time, they played on the pitch opposite the one they used in later years. It might have been when they opened the new ground. Enderby always had a beauty queen – Doris Smith (Harrison) was one and Kath Wallace was another. One year, Don Revie came to crown the queen.

B.T.

Stan Mortimer, Jonny Walker and Mr Drummond with the FA Cup, 4 September 1957.

Stan Matthews visits Enderby Co-op, 1957.

Lost cricket ball

I was playing once with Enderby second team at Sapcote. I remember that I hit a ball not many yards off the square and we ran seven. What happened was, they couldn't find the ball, as it was in a hole, under a dried cow pat! I remember many of the players – there were three brothers, Jack, Alf and Cis West, Albert Wright, Billy Poyner, Cliff Taylor, Albert Charles, Horace Spence, Ernie Gilliver and Teddy Knight. There was another thing about Enderby Cricket Club, you had to be an Enderby resident, or married and come to live in the village, to be allowed to play. One chap who married an Enderby girl and came to live here was called Jayes. I played there for some thirty-four years and really enjoyed it.

Roy Coulson

Kick-off at the opening of the new football ground, Aston Villa v. Enderby Town. From left to right: Tony Shields, Mr Drummond and Nev Duncan, 4 September 1957.

Medals

Enderby Town won the Senior League and District League ten years on the trot. I've got the medals to show for it. I've got 138 altogether! Enderby Town had a very good District League side and they won the Senior Cup a few times. We used to go to matches together on a bus. Mellors' bus used to pick us up from the Co-op. We were well looked after in those days

Lenny Fawell

Cricket crowds

I hope I brought a bit of humour to the *Journal* with sporting photos. One of my favourites was of the old men who gathered at the corner of Bantlam Lane to watch the cricket matches. The caption was 'Rumours that Enderby Cricket Club is getting bigger crowds than Enderby Town are to be investigated'. Most village pubs put up that picture.

Mark Postlethwaite

Captain Drummond's team

While I was playing for Enderby, we used to have two matches a season against Scraptoft Valley. A.T. Sharpe looked after their team, and Captain Drummond looked after the Enderby team. Captain Drummond paid for the beer and sandwiches at Enderby, and A.T. Sharpe paid when we went there.

Roy Coulson

The well-known crowd photograph.

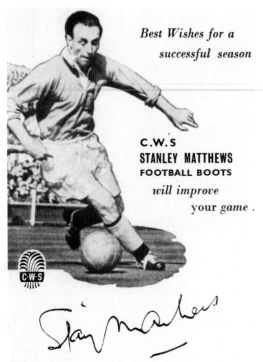

Best Wishes for a
successful season

C.W.S
STANLEY MATTHEWS
FOOTBALL BOOTS
will improve
your game .

All sizes in stock for men and boys at
YOUR CO-OPERATIVE SOCIETY

Left: *A Co-op advert for Stanley Matthews football boots; a copy of a postcard signed by him on a visit to Enderby Co-op, 1957.*

Left below: *Horace Jacques with Stan Matthews at Enderby Town football ground, 1957.*

Past cricketers

As I remember, the cricket was played down Mill Lane. We had some good members when I first started playing there, and, of them, Lou Harris and Albert Charles are still alive now. The captain was Viv North, who was an excellent player. We used to practise cricket on a Friday night to get ready for Saturday's match. Years ago, when I played cricket, you had to be born in Enderby to play for the club, which was a good thing.

Lenny Fawell

Enderby Town floodlights

I once heard that Enderby's facilities were the best in the Southern League. The pitch was immaculate – a superb pitch. My brother claims the distinction of being the first player to score a goal under the floodlights, as just after the lights were fitted, my brother and I went down with Dad and had a go on the pitch while the lights were on. We had a kick about in the goal and my brother was the first to score. The lights were put up in the sixties, and were designed for a very high standard of football. It seemed as though the club had plenty of money to be able to buy what they wanted. The club was a real family thing for me – my mother worked in the refreshment bar, my father was the groundsman, then became the secretary, my grandfather was chairman, and my uncle Barry was also connected with the club. We lived and breathed the football club.

Mark Postlethwaite

eight
Village Life

Blaby Board of Guardians, Enderby Workhouse, 1911.

Taking in the strays

When I was a little nipper, I could nip about a bit. The thing I remember most is that I loved dogs. If I went anywhere and there were any dogs, roaming the streets, as they did then, I'd take them home. I'd hide it, but my mother would come in and say, 'It's got to go, you can't keep it here'. I did that for years.

Sadie Jayes

The picture house

We used to have a picture place. We used to call it the Gadget. It was a wooden building opposite where Barclays Bank is now in Broad Street. They were real actors, but of course they weren't very good. We used to shout. I remember one, it was a serial and it was called The Mystery Rider. When that was on, my friend was in the hospital with scarlet fever. I used to have to go to the picture house and watch this film, and then write

her a letter. I would only be about eleven, if that. Then Chestertons came and had a picture place. That was where Holt's factory was, the wood yard.

D.L.

Plough Inn, Mill Hill.

The price of a pint

I can remember the price of a pint being as low as fourpence, then sixpence and up to ninepence, but when it got to a shilling, everyone was outraged. I used to play darts for a tanner a time. I used to buy a glass of beer, play darts all evening and then realise my glass of beer was still there, flat as a pancake! Then there was dominoes, cards and a bit of cribbage, they were the main things. There was Ray Cox and a chap with one eye, they'd go round all the pubs playing darts, and it was quite a challenge when they came to the Havelock. It were a treat to beat them!

Jeff Steer

Mr Chesterton's cinema

It was marvellous for us to have the cinema. No one in the villages round here had a cinema at all. The funny thing was, Mr Chesterton, who owned the cinema, also owned one at Barlestone. We had one film while they had another, and then in the interval, they swapped round. They drove to a certain spot and swapped the films. It was absolutely wonderful, because there weren't many places that had a cinema. Really, Enderby was what I would call a prosperous village, because it had lots of shops apart from the Co-op, and they all made a living.

Mary Cox

Ladies fellowship

The ladies fellowship, of which I am a member, has been going for many, many years. I've only been a member for a few years, but I can remember my aunts being members, and they're long gone. It was a very strong society, they did good works, and there was a meeting once a week. We have a president, these last few years it has been Mrs Sheila

Dorothy Cherry, aged three, with her grandfather, right, who was landlord of the Plough Inn.

Maides, and I am vice-president. We're all official, with a secretary and a treasurer. We meet every other Tuesday now, starting at three o'clock, and we have the usual – that is, the Methodist sandwich. We have a hymn, a prayer, a hymn and a reading chosen by the speaker. It's not all biblical talks, they're real funny, some of them. John Lane is coming soon, and Margaret Gillespie comes too. The meeting goes on for about an hour, then it's the inevitable cup of tea and biscuits afterwards. This group has been going for many years, and has been a great asset to the church, especially financially. They give a good amount to the church, which every group needs to do to cover its costs of heating and lighting and so on, and they have a special

The cover of the C.W.S. fashion catalogue, 1938.

King William IV pub and Folly Cottages, 1970.

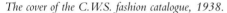

weekend each year, usually in March, when they hold a coffee morning and then have a special Sunday service, usually with a visiting lady speaker. They look after those who are not well, and they have a pastoral care section to care for members of the church. We are not a 'closed shop' – people from the 'big' church, the parish church, can come, and we often join forces with the United Reform church, who are only a small group. We've got about twenty-odd members, which is not bad for a small village. We invite the U.R.C. people to come on our outings, and they join us for our Christmas party. Yes, it's quite an asset to our church.

Jean Carter

Household conveniences

There was three toilets between five houses at the top of the yard, which was a 'pan' toilet, it didn't flush. It was emptied every Monday

morning by a bloke named Horace Spence, who drove the lorry, and a bloke named Cliff Palmer. Cliff was a great lad, but people took the mickey out of him a bit. These two emptied the muck pans for a couple of days a week, then they'd go back to emptying the dustbins. In them days, the dustbins were emptied down 'the Hardwicke', which is now Forest Road. They just tipped what they'd fetched out of the toilets down there as well, just had a big hole and gradually filled it in, then they'd make a new hole. It came down to where the football field was, the one they've just done away with.

Nigel Cooper

Enderby old folks' entertainment fund

At the end of the last war, there were a number of gentlemen who enjoyed each other's company, maybe in the pub, and they got together to do something for the village for the end of the war. They decided to have a party for the old folk – after all, they, their sons and husbands had been in the war. So they put on a tea in the Co-op Hall, which was in Co-operation Street, and it was a great success. By the way, they had gone begging everywhere for the food, nothing was bought, and they put on a wonderful tea. They decided to make it an annual event, and a committee was set up ready for the next year. Arthur Capers was made chairman, a position he held until he passed away, well into his nineties. They decided that a good way to entertain the old folk was to take them out on a coach, and this has led to annual outings of two half-days and one full-day. The committee was all men, on the principal that it was good for men to organise something like this, and if you got a man involved, you almost certainly got his wife as well! In more recent years, we have put on other things as well as the annual tea and outings. Now there is a concert party of professional artistes organised by Les Wilson. He gives his time free, and brings to Enderby acts he has met during the summer season for a two-hour concert. Ernie Jarvis, a committee member, was concerned about those people who didn't come to the events, and he went on to organise the Enderby tote. He and Joe Illson made such a success of this that we were able to give everyone eligible (men over sixty-five and ladies over sixty) ten shillings(fifty pence) and later this went up to a pound. A nice gesture was to give it with a Christmas card, so that all the old folk were bound to get at least one Christmas card. We felt the card was just as important as the pound. We've kept that up and two years ago we celebrated fifty years of service to the old folk of Enderby. We get huge support from the village, especially the shops and businesses, who so willingly donate gifts for the prize draw. We also get a good deal of money from the regular bingo sessions.

Frank Humphrey

Pennies for a nurse

My mother was secretary of the Nursing Association, and she would go round the village every week and collect pennies to pay for a district nurse. Then, when anyone had a baby, the nurse would attend. All those pennies paid for her. There was no National Health Service, you'd pay the doctor a fee. When the National Health Service came in, my father was a life governor of Leicester Royal, and he came home from the last meeting and his comment was, 'Well, they've got the lot'. He said that the government had taken everything. I think, in a roundabout way, all the governors were upset, they'd lost the cause they supported. Father was also a guardian of Enderby House. When we were small, we all used to troop down to the harvest festival there.

Molly Broomhall and JoyceTurner

Christmas as a child

I used to get an orange, a Rupert book and a few chocolates if I was lucky for Christmas. The Co-op used to have a drapery section, and they used to set the windows out lovely with all the glittery stuff. As a kid, you used to go and stand and look in that window and just wish that you could have some of the things you could see, but you knew damned well you wouldn't get them because you couldn't afford them.

Norma Hall

Enderby flower club

About forty-five years ago, a group of people decided they would like to meet to arrange flowers, and the group went on from there. We meet every month. We've decorated churches, chapels, done exhibitions, and we are quite a big club now. I once worked with Gladys Powell giving classes at the Woodlands Day Centre to help some of the patients prepare to come back into the community.

Jenny Smith

St John's nightlarks

Just after the war, Bill Salt, who used to run the nursery across the road from us in John Street, was also a bell-ringer. He and I got talking one night and we decided to form a concert party. I was the pianist and compère, and we also involved Fred Spence and George Clarke. We called ourselves the St John's Nightlarks, and we used to do a concert every year in the Co-op Hall. It used to run for three nights. Monday was always a full rehearsal, then the concert was on for the next three nights. Fred Spence used to sell the tickets in the newsagents, and they were always sold out by mid-morning of the first day they were available.

Herbert Gilliver

Top Chapel playgroup

I had my son and stopped work, and when he was about three months old, I realised that I couldn't stay at home all day. I needed something to do. I talked with my friend, Josie, who had two small children, and we discussed playgroups. We went round to visit a few, and then decided that we could run one ourselves. We filled in all the necessary forms, and when we were approved, the chapel said we could use the church hall. We brought in another member from the church, Sheila Young, and the three of us started the playgroup at the chapel, in about 1970. There were a few

A page from the C.W.S. fashion catalogue, 1938.

groups starting up in villages, but it was quite a new idea really. Because Josie was a teacher and I was a nurse, the authorities accepted us, but now there are special qualifications needed to run a playgroup. Even so, we had to be registered with the council, and had to have various checks.

Judith North

A 'ten-shilling widow'

I was born in Huncote, and we came to Enderby when I was five years old. My dad died when I was five, and my mum was what they called a 'ten-shilling widow'. That's all the widow's pension she got because she was too young when my dad died. Her mother and sister lived in Enderby, so we moved here to be nearer to them. They lived right next door to the Methodist chapel, where Kwik-Save is now. Their house was knocked down to build the Kwik-Save building. We lived up in Chapel Street – those houses have gone now too. There was a yard with about four houses, opposite the top chapel.

Alan Smith

Journal headlines

I joined the *Journal* when I was about twelve, mainly to get into the photography side. I started on the *Junior Journal* where I did my drawings and cartoons. It was great fun in those days on Saturdays, when it was layout time. We had Chris Gane, Sally Anderson, Liz Harrold (Durrance now), and Andy Seaton. He was such a funny chap. He came up with some fantastic headlines, but we couldn't use many of them! I remember once that a vicar died, and the headline we wanted to use was 'Promoted to Head Office'. Another time was when Billy Whitmore's shoe repairers was turned into a building society, and we wanted to use 'Cobblers to building society'! On layout days, we'd send someone up to the chippy at lunchtime and we'd have masses of chips and fish – it was a real social event. In the early days, we did the collation by hand in the council offices above Forget-Me-Knot. It wasn't a popular job. You'd just have tables filled with each page, and you'd have to walk along and take one of each page until you had them all, then carefully fold them in half. Because no-one wanted to do that job, it could be real hard work. In the end, I think I was on the board when it was finally decided to get it collated professionally. I then went on to edit *Junior Journal*, taking it in turns with Mark Jennings, Joanne Hall, Sally Yates and Andy Orton. When I was about sixteen, I got my first 35mm camera, and together with Mark Jennings, we learned all about photography from the *Journal* photographer, John Byrne. He'd had years of experience. Mark and I became photographers for the *Journal*. My photographs formed my portfolio, and with that, I got a job in photography, which lasted for ten years. We went on to edit the *Journal* for about a year or so.

Mark Postlethwaite

Cosy cinema

The Cosy cinema had two programmes a week. The local chimney sweep, Joe Green, used to play the piano, he was a brilliant pianist. It was pretty good for a small village.

Mavis Almond

Joining the Women's Institute with a hat!

I can always remember my mother-in-law, Marjorie Thorpe, saying to me when the children were born, 'You'll need time out on your own. It doesn't matter where you go, as long as it's time for yourself.' I've never forgotten that, and that's how I came to join the Women's Institute. We used to meet once a month in the Co-op Hall, then we moved to Brockington school, and finally to the village institute. After my first baby in 1967, I was with the W.I. for about ten years when the president, Dorothy Humphreys, retired. Instead of the vice-president taking over, they decided to hold a ballot, and, horror of horrors, yours truly got elected. I came home and told my husband that I'd landed this job, something I'd never done before, but I must say, the committee and everyone else were very supportive. In those days, you didn't go to a W.I. meeting without a hat on, and you had to dress up for group meetings. Fortunately, I had plenty of hats! I can remember going to the Albert Hall, to the annual general meeting. It was a wonderful experience to hear *Jerusalem* sung in the Albert Hall, and to see all those hats of all shapes and colours.

Sheila Thorpe

Mobile cinema

When we lived on the Cross, there was one of these here mobile wagons, a picture house. When they opened the doors at the back they had a screen just inside, and you'd have Felix cartoons. Those sort of films, they were only short. It was all free. You could stand outside the Conservative Club and watch them.

Laurence Lilley

The prefabs

I remember the prefabs being built. They had prisoners of war digging the footings out, and I remember one of them asking my friend over the road to help him learn to speak English. The buildings came in two halves on great lorries. They were great really, quite well designed. People quite took to them. When they had to come down to make way for

brick-built bungalows, a lot of people were quite upset.

Joyce Fawell

Infirmary beds

There used to be a fête every year in the grounds of Enderby Hall in the years leading up to the war. The whole village was involved in this because the aim was to raise money to endow a bed at the Royal Infirmary. The ladies in the village would go round knocking on doors, and people very generously gave a

ENDERBY & LUBBESTHORPE BED FUND COMMITTEE.
Chairman: Mr. H. A. JACKSON.
Hon. Secretary: Mr. G. HALL.
Hon. Treasurer: Mr. P. E. TIMMINS.

1928.	No. 1 Bed.	Rogers Ward.
1933.	No. 2 Bed.	Odames Ward.
1933.	No. 1 Cot.	Hall of Children's Hospital.
1943.	No. 3 Bed.	Apreece Ward.

SATURDAY, NOVEMBER 3rd, 1945, at 2.10 p.m.

Order of Service for the Dedication of the Enderby & Lubbesthorpe Bed No. 4, endowed by the Parishioners in the sum of £1,000.

Friends will assemble in the Board Room and will then be conducted to the Balcony of Froane Ward.

HYMN.

We give Thee but Thine own,
Whate'er the gift may be:
All that we have is Thine alone,
A trust, O Lord, from Thee.

To comfort and to bless,
To find a balm for woe,
To tend the lone and fatherless,
Is Angels' work below.

May we Thy bounties thus
As stewards true receive,
And gladly, as Thou blessest us,
To Thee our first-fruits give.

The captive to release,
To God the lost to bring,
To teach the way of life and peace,
It is a Christ-like thing.

Oh, hearts are bruised and dead,
And homes are bare and cold,
And lambs, for whom the
Shepherd bled,
Are straying from the fold.

And we believe Thy Word,
Though dim our faith may be;
Whate'er for Thine we do, O Lord,
We do it unto Thee.

All might, all praise be Thine,
Father, Co-equal Son,
And Spirit, Bond of love Divine,
While endless ages run.

Enderby Conservative Club, the Cross, formerly reading rooms and coffee house, built 1872.

The dedication of the Enderby bed in Leicester Royal Infirmary, 3 November 1945.

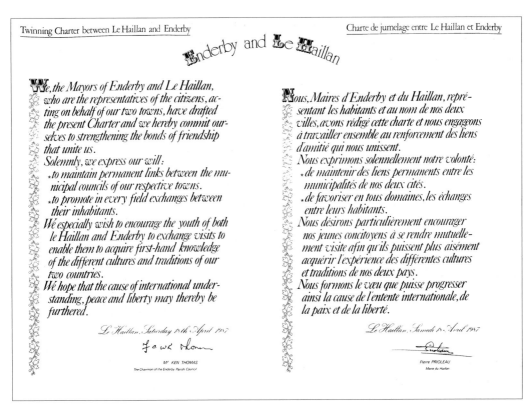

Twinning Charter between Le Haillan and Enderby

Charte de jumelage entre Le Haillan et Enderby

Enderby and Le Haillan

We, the Mayors of Enderby and Le Haillan, who are the representatives of the citizens, acting on behalf of our two towns, have drafted the present Charter and we hereby commit ourselves to strengthening the bonds of friendship that unite us.

Solemnly, we express our will:
. to maintain permanent links between the municipal councils of our respective towns.
. to promote in every field exchanges between their inhabitants.

We especially wish to encourage the youth of both le Haillan and Enderby to exchange visits to enable them to acquire first-hand knowledge of the different cultures and traditions of our two countries.

We hope that the cause of international understanding, peace and liberty may thereby be furthered.

Le Haillan, Saturday 18th April 1987

Mr KEN THOMAS
The Chairman of the Enderby Parish Council

Nous, Maires d'Enderby et du Haillan, représentant les habitants et au nom de nos deux villes, avons rédigé cette charte et nous engageons à travailler ensemble au renforcement des liens d'amitié qui nous unissent.

Nous exprimons solennellement notre volonté:
. de maintenir des liens permanents entre les municipalités de nos deux cités.
. de favoriser en tous domaines, les échanges entre leurs habitants.

Nous désirons particulièrement encourager nos jeunes concitoyens à se rendre mutuellement visite afin qu'ils puissent plus aisément acquérir l'expérience des différentes cultures et traditions de nos deux pays.

Nous formons le vœu que puisse progresser ainsi la cause de l'entente internationale, de la paix et de la liberté.

Le Haillan, Samedi 18 Avril 1987

Pierre PRIOLEAU
Maire du Haillan

The twinning charter for Enderby and Le Haillan, 1987.

pound of sugar or half-a-pound of butter, or a cake for the refreshments. There was a teacher at the junior school who was extremely good at making up concerts. She used to devise a concert that involved everyone from the school, and that was performed at the fête. I think there were also races for the children. I know it was very well-attended, and there would be a carnival queen and her attendants who would be chosen beforehand. When a certain amount of money had been raised, a thousand pounds, there would be the dedication of a plaque over a bed in one of the wards to say who had raised the money. We were just one of the villages who did this in order to put extra money into our local hospital.

Claire Timmins

Housing

The biggest changes in Enderby were the housing estates like the one round Coleridge Drive. Before this was built, when you left the village going down Seine Lane, you were onto fields, or what we called 'the Breach', at the back of the top chapel. You were onto fields until you got to Huncote. It was bounded by the old railway line that came up from Narborough station to the quarry. That was the old mineral railway that's now a footpath called Whistle Way.

Derek Brooks

Cosy cinema

There was the Cosy cinema at the back of where Kwik-Save is now, in Townsend Road.

It was a converted cowshed. I used to pal about a bit with a man that helped Mr Chesterton of the Granby cinema, and Ronald Hearsey, who lived in Strawberry Gardens, in Bradley's old nursery. Ronald used to look after the sound equipment up there. It was one single sloping floor, and you went in at the side of the screen, through the pay box. I always remember when it was time for the film to start, whoever was in the pay box would wind a handle to open the curtains across the screen, and dim the lights – there was a dimmer switch on the wall at the side. At a guess, it would hold about two hundred and fifty. The seats right at the front were just a wooden form and the younger kids would go in them. The better seats went back. I think it was about sixpence to sit at the front, and it wasn't much more than a shilling or maybe two bob to sit in the better seats. They were all black and white cowboy films with Gene Autrey and Roy Rogers, and comic films with Charlie Chaplin and George Formby.

Derek Brooks

Enderby twinning with Le Haillan. Monsieur Prioleau and Ken Thomas, spring 1987.

Twinning

While I was chairman of the parish council, the principal of Brockington College, Tom King, and the deputy, Laurie Maries, attended a council meeting. They told us that the local municipality at Le Haillan (near Bordeaux in France) was looking for a town in this country to 'twin' with. Tom King was afraid that if they didn't find somewhere around the Enderby area, the school exchange between Brockington and Collège Emile Zola in Le Haillan, which had taken place each year since 1980, would be threatened. The parish council decided to investigate the possibility of twinning with Le Haillan to safeguard the exchange. In 1982, my wife and I, along with Colin Richardson (clerk to Enderby Parish Council) and his wife, went down to Le Haillan to meet the mayor and other members of the council. They explained that Le Haillan was about the same distance from Bordeaux as Enderby was from Leicester, and a bit more industrialised. We came back and recommended that we go ahead with the twinning. Before my trip there, I didn't know where it was. We had several public meetings to see what Enderby people thought of the twinning idea. Eventually, in 1987, we went down to Le Haillan and signed the twinning agreement. The following year, their people came over to Enderby and the agreement was also signed here. To be quite honest, from about half-a-dozen people being involved at the start, it has now grown to a membership of over fifty. We visit from here one year, and the French members come here the following year. We all enjoy our visits, and it's really opened my eyes. Sadly, the school exchange is becoming difficult to arrange because of tighter regulations regarding school trips, but the twinning is thriving.

Ken Thomas

British Legion

In the late fifties, I was more interested in the social side of the British Legion, and, having helped Mr Griffin with his standard bearing display, he wanted me to help him with the British Legion. I volunteered to organise the dances. Carlton Hayes Hospital used to have so many dances a year, and allowed the British Legion to have two of these to add to their funds. In those days, these two dances were our main source of income. The poppy appeal

money goes straight to Pall Mall (headquarters) so that provides no local income. Sadly, the secretary of the Enderby branch of the British Legion, Doug Thompson, passed away, so I went to one meeting as social secretary, and came away as branch secretary as well. I held that job until the closure of the Enderby branch a couple of years ago.

Frank Humphrey

Festival of remembrance

Each year, we send the application form to Pall Mall, and we usually get two tickets allocated to Enderby to attend the evening performance at the Royal Albert Hall. You can apply for your branch standard to appear, but there's only four, maximum, Leicestershire standards can appear. Not so long ago, Paul Kurganovas was invited from our branch.

Frank Humphrey

The British Legion beauty queen and her attendants.

Celebrating the fiftieth anniversary of VJ Day. From left to right:, Paul Kurganovas, Bob Johnson RN, Bill Wenlock, Burma Star Organisation, Jean Mercer, Jimmy Harrison RAF and ex-Leicester City FC.

Frank Humphrey, branch chairman, British Legion, laying up the standard in Enderby church, 1 September 2000.

Closure of the Enderby branch

I was so disappointed when the Enderby branch closed and our standard was laid up in the church. I so wanted Paul to take that standard. We arranged a band concert with Enderby band at the church for the laying up ceremony, but Paul Kurganovas had a holiday booked, so we had to have a deputy standard-bearer. It was a wonderful evening, though rather a sentimental occasion, the end of an era. Now there are four standards in Enderby church, two on either side of the memorial.

Frank Humphrey

Local councillor

In 1972, there was a vacancy in St John's ward for a representative on what was then Blaby Rural District Council, and there was a man standing for it who lived in Kirby Muxloe. I thought 'Well, blow me, you don't want someone representing St John's who lives in Kirby Muxloe', so I decided to stand as an Independent. I was elected, and for seventeen years, I served on Blaby District Council. For sixteen of those years, I was on the planning committee, and in 1983-4, I was chairman.

Ken Thomas

Bradley's market garden

My mother was a Spence, and her grandfather was Arthur Freestone, who used to keep the Black Horse down Seine Lane. My dad worked down Bradley's market garden, just before where Hawgrip nurseries is now, just over the quarry railway line. He worked there for many a year, and then, all of a sudden, Mr Bradley sold up and a man called Mr Hearsey took over. After a few years, he said he couldn't afford my father, so he went to work for Jones and Shipman until he passed away when he was fifty-six.

Stuart Buzzard

Christmas football

We never got out very far at Christmas because there was no transport. We had our festivities either at home or with our grandparents. We'd have dinner in one place, then have tea in the other. In those days, football teams used to play a fixture on Christmas morning, then play the return match on Boxing Day. We used to go down to Filbert Street. Sometimes, there'd be a coach run by Bob Phillips, sometimes, we'd walk, down through Aylestone, by the canal, to Filbert Street. If we could, we'd try to get a lift back on the coach. The buses never came to Enderby until the late thirties.

B.T.

Local structure plan

In the Leicestershire structure plan, Blaby District Council was supposed to allocate a hundred acres for industrial development near the M1 slip road, so they allocated the land where Fosse Park is now, because the land where Meridian is now was held up because the ministry was going to build a flyover over the M1 onto the M69. At that time, there wasn't a lot of take-up for industrial development, but Asda made an application to build a store there and this was eventually approved. That single application opened the door for what is now Fosse Park. Earlier on, planning permission had been turned down for development of the Grove park site.

Ken Thomas

The Jubes

The old Enderby picture house wasn't very big, they called it 'Jubes'. It was at the side of Holt's factory in Brook Street. The back entrance was opposite the old Co-op garage, and the British Legion was next door. They were mostly like bench seats. The first two rows were fivepence, the next two or three rows went up to sevenpence. Then you'd get the plush fold-up and down seats. Some of these were either tenpence or a shilling, and then up at the back they were one and nine. There were old Cagney films, cartoons, cowboys and the Movietone news.

Jeff Steer

Mill Lane allotments

The allotments were owned by the Oddfellows, and holders used to subscribe to the Manchester Friendly Society. They used to meet up at the New Inn to pay the subscriptions. In the early days, the allotments were where the leisure centre is now. My

Allotment holders in the 1980s.

granddad had a plot down there, and I used to go and dig it for him. Eventually, they moved further down Mill Lane, to where they are now.

B.T.

Pigeons

My dad kept pigeons, racing pigeons. Well, we weren't very happy about that really because my sister and my eldest brother and me had to help dad get the pigeons in, in the loft, when they flew from places like Banff in Scotland. When it was our turn, we couldn't go until all the pigeons were in and ringed, and it didn't go down ever so well, but we were ever so proud when he won his cups and things like that.

Jean Carter

Before the houses were built

I lived down George Street, and at the bottom of there was Sludge Alley. That went over to West Street and the other side of the road was allotments. Further on down, there was a stackyard (farmyard), and on the other side Mr Jesson had his allotment. It was all allotments down there, and on our deeds, it says the land belonged to the Co-op who then sold it to

Winsons. If you carried on down, through another stackyard, you came to the tip, where the playing fields at the back of Kipling Drive are now. Years before that, there was a brick-works on that corner.

Clive Hall

The time capsule

The *Leicester Mercury* ran a competition for W.I.s, and one year, it was to create a time capsule with ten items in it. I can't remember all the things we put in, but we included Nigel Lawson's budget speech (he was chancellor at the time, and the local MP), a pint milk bottle, because there was talk of doing away with milkmen, and one of the early disposable nappies. Anyway, we won the competition, and had to go to De Montfort Hall to collect a silver plate.

Sheila Thorpe

Allotments

My grandfather had an allotment in Federation Street, as did my father. When I was a little girl, I remember going down there and setting peas. My father was a hard taskmaster, everything had to be done just right. During the war, we used to 'dig for victory', as it were, and helped each other out with what we grew. You could leave your doors open, it was quite safe in those days.

Jenny Smith

Wakes fair

The wakes fair was always held at the back of the Plough Inn on Mill Hill. They had chair-o'-planes, a waltzer, and a cake-walk. You went up and down as you tried to walk along that. And there were swing boats.

Mavis Almond

Left: *Enderby Wakes Fair, Mill Lane recreation ground, early 1980s*

Below: *Brookes' shop on the Cross, with a poster in the window for the Cosy cinema advertising John Mills in Morning Departure, 1951.*

Two films a week

There was the Cosy cinema, and that used to have two different films on a week, one on Monday, Tuesday and Wednesday, the other on Thursday, Friday and Saturday. There was always a supporting programme, it was usually a cowboy. Inside they used to have benches that cost fivepence (2p). If you paid seven-pence, you got a bench with foam on it, but the kids picked most of that off so there wasn't much left. Then the shilling (5p) seats were tip-up ones and further back were the one and nines – they were great! There wasn't a lot really for us to do, only the pubs and the club. I went to the guides for a little while, but they were going camping and that cost money and we hadn't got much.

Joyce Fawell

The WI heart machine

The WI always did some charity work. The year before I became president, we supported mentally handicapped children. Christian Barnard had just performed the first heart transplant, and I wanted to do something to benefit a lot of people, so I suggested some sort of heart machine. I went to see Doctor Brown to ask what he thought we could get for about £100, and he suggested a resuscitation machine would be a good idea. The committee thought this was a good idea, so we set out to raise what seemed like a huge amount of money. The whole village became involved, and within eighteen months, we'd got not £100, but £250, so we could provide a much bigger machine. Just before the end of our fund-raising for that, we had a concert put on by Les Wilson, the comedian, at Brockington school. Doctor Goldberg, the heart specialist, was presented with the cheque, and we went to the hospital to see the machine working.

Sheila Thorpe

Making our own fun

We used to make our own entertainment. All the children learned how to play a musical instrument, and a lot of them were members of the band. My mother used to take us wherever dad was playing, and we'd take a picnic and sit and listen to them playing. They played a lot at Wicksteed Park, and at all the fêtes and parades in the village and at the hall.

Jenny Smith

Don Revie crowns the queen

Years ago, the village had a parade in the summer, and one year, Don Revie, the old Leicester City player, was invited to crown the village beauty queen.

Lenny Fawell

Keeping the kids amused

There was only the Cosy cinema and the youth club at the school to keep the youngsters amused. Kids nowadays say there's nothing to do in the village, but in those days, we really did have very little. We used to play 'hare and hounds' round the streets.

Clive Hall

The Enderby bed

There was a fête every year, it always coincided with the collection for Queen Alexandra's Rose Day. It was always in the park, and there was a procession round the village beforehand. The money raised from the fête was used to endow a bed, the Enderby

---

SCRIPTURE READING.
The Rev. W. Simpson.

The Rev. H. V. Hibbert will dedicate the Bed in the following words:—

In the name of the Father and of the Son and of the Holy Ghost. Amen.

To the Glory of God and to the service of humanity, I dedicate this Bed endowed by the Parishioners of Enderby and Lubbesthorpe, and may the occupants of this Bed under the merciful providenc of God be restored to health of body, mind and soul and to lives of usefulness and service. Amen.

PRAYER.

The Unveiling Ceremony will be performed by
Mr. P. E. TIMMINS,
who will read the inscription above the Bed as follows:—

ENDERBY & LUBBESTHORPE
BED No. 4.
ENDOWED AS A TRIBUTE TO THE WORK OF THE INFIRMARY THROUGH THE EFFORTS OF THE PARISH UNDER THE ORGANISATION OF THE BRITISH LEGION.
Chairman: Mr. H. A. JACKSON,
Hon. Secretary: Mr. G. HALL.
Hon. Treasurer: Mr. P. E. TIMMINS.
1945

BENEDICTION.

RETURN TO BOARD ROOM.

INFIRMARY INSPECTION.

Order of service for the dedication of the Enderby bed, 3 November 1945.

bed, at the royal infirmary. Of course, this was before the National Health Service. The infirmary relied on these beds, and many villages used to provide one.

Mavis Almond

W.I. and the undertaker!

We had competitions and demonstrations at our meetings, and many guest speakers. One of the funniest was when an undertaker came, and, instead of it being a solemn occasion, he had them rolling in the aisles.

Sheila Thorpe

The Enderby walk

There used to be a ten-mile walk, I think it was the *Mercury* walk, that used to go from Enderby Hall down past Len's (my husband's) mum's house on Mill Hill. I don't know where they went for the rest of the ten miles. In the late forties, a man called Mr Johnson used to win it a lot.

Joyce Fawell

Presents in your stocking

On Christmas morning, you'd get an orange, an apple, a few nuts, a comic album (maybe *Rainbow*, *Picturegoer* or *Comic Cuts*), and maybe a small toy. The Co-op used to have a Christmas toy fair above their offices with Santa.

B.T.

First film

The Cosy Corner was situated between Holt's factory and the Enderby club, (before it moved down to Coleridge Drive). I think it opened in the 1930s, and the first film was Jessie Matthews in *Evergreen*. I was at the junior school, and we went for a free show-

ing. There was always a 'B' movie as well as the main picture. The fellow that owned the cinema was a Mr Chesterton. It used to be fourpence in the front seats, then sixpence, ninepence and a shilling at the back. They had double seats in the back row. Eventually, they had tip-up seats. Mr Chesterton had another cinema in Barlestone, and they used to have one film at the beginning of the week in Enderby, and the end of the week in Barlestone, and vice-versa. On Saturdays, there would be a first and second house. That cinema was a blessing for the village during the war years.

B.T.

Hearing the band

I was walking past the junior school and I could hear this music. I wondered what it was. I was only seven, so I crept up the steps and along the corridor and came to this door where I could hear the music. The bottom half of the door was frosted glass, and only the top half was plain, so I started jumping up to see through the plain glass. Somebody saw me, one of the bandsmen, and he told the conductor, who stopped the band and came through the door. He said, ' Do you like brass band music, sonny?' I told him I did, so he told me to come in and sit at the back and listen. So that's what I did.

Ernie Yeomanson

Spitting the tea leaf

When the band had a break, the conductor took me into another room where there was an old brass cornet and asked me if I wanted to play it. He told me how to tongue it, 'spit the tea leaf off your tongue' sort of thing, and I got quite a good note. He told me to take the cornet home and keep doing that, and to

ENDERBY TOWN SILVER PRIZE BAND, 1936.

Enderby band, 1936. Ernie Yeomanson is back row, second left.

come back next week. I about drove my mum and dad daft! I went back the next week, and got quite a good tone, so he wrote the scale out for me up to 'c'. He got me playing that, and then sent me off for another week to practise. After that, I got to play *O God, Our Help In Ages Past* and then I was in the junior band with Dennis Darby and that lot. I played with them until I were about twelve, and then they put me in the band at third cornet. I gradually worked my way up until I played alongside Tommy Smith, solo.

Ernie Yeomanson

Melton and chips

I was sixteen when I went to play at Melton early one morning. It was a Midlands contest, with bands from Snibston, Wigston, Enderby and all around, and we played in the afternoon, a march and a selection. We got back into Belgrave Gate at turned midnight, and some-body mentioned a fish and chip shop. We'd had a drink, and I was only sixteen. We all piled out and went to this chip shop, and he was just finished for the night, just cleaning up. Well, the pan was still hot, so we said to him 'Get the pan on', and he put in another load of chips for us. We got back to Enderby at about half-past-one. I had a bit of a snooze on the settee, then we had to be at the King William at half-past-seven to have our photo taken.

Ernie Yeomanson

Start of Enderby Band

At one time there were two bands in Enderby. We certainly know that there was a temperance band in the mid to late 1800s, but the band that we now know as Enderby Band was formed, we thought, in 1895, because we celebrated the centenary in 1995. However, from conversations with John Freestone about his family, we think the band was founded slightly

Enderby band, 1931.

before that, in 1893. Two of the founder members were Job Biggs, who was my great-great grandfather, and his son, Herbert Biggs. Whether it was just an offshoot of the temperance band or a rival group, I'm not sure, or whether they were backsliders, we don't actually know. The temperance band faded out and the non-temperance band flourished.

Garry Sleath

Carols with the band

My first memory of the band is coming round on Christmas morning playing carols. Before the war the band used to go out during the evening and play over the night, then go and collect the money in the morning (Christmas Day), but after the war it changed. I remember the band coming round playing carols on Christmas morning, and coming in for a tot of whisky or sherry and a mince pie.

Garry Sleath

Rehearsing at the pub

I also remember the band rehearsing in the old social club, which was where the Dog and Gun car park is now, next to the Cosy cinema. They used to rehearse there in the late 1950s and early 1960s. In fact, they've rehearsed at most of the licensed premises in the village over the years – the New Inn skittle alley, the Havelock tap-room and so on. In the early days we didn't have a practice room, so we rehearsed in my father's back yard at 18 Townsend Road. My father rigged up some temporary lights and the band had to rehearse there. I remember hearing one of the neighbours saying, 'One of the Sleaths didn't half have their radio turned up loud the other night'.

Garry Sleath

My first engagement, and no music!

I do remember my first engagement with the band. I must have been about ten, and we

John Sleath selling raffle tickets in the band centenary year, 1995.

Garry Sleath. Band headquarters at 32 The Nook, 1963.

were playing at what was a Hinckley Sunday schools treats march in the early sixties. It was a huge parade. The bands went down into The Borough, and the crowds on either side were enormous. They had these big floats with different themes, and at various points they had bands. It was a very long parade so they had three or four bands. I was given a lift there by a cornet player called Stan Hearne, who is still playing horn in the county. We were late getting there and because of the crowd you just couldn't get through. So there we were, him and me and another youngster, trying to get in to play. We had to push our way through the crowds to get to the top of The Borough. My grandfather was waiting, looking out for us. We got to a point where we could sneak in at the back of the band as they came past. Because Stan was playing solo cornet, it was important that he got the music, so they got the music to him. I said to my grandfather 'I haven't got any

music', so he replied 'just keep playing Gs'. For the whole of the march I played offbeat Gs. It didn't matter what key the band was in. I must have played 250 Gs on my first engagement.

Garry Sleath

The price of a wife

The family line has run through the band right from the beginning. My grandfather, Arthur William (Dick) Biggs, was a local shoe repairer and he gave me my first lesson on the cornet in his workshop at 32 The Nook. My father, John, was the secretary. There is a story that when he asked for my mother's hand in marriage, my grandfather replied, 'You can have her as long as you agree to become secretary'. So my father took on the job of secretary and the headquarters were at 32 The Nook. These houses were later pulled down, so they moved to 18 Townsend Road.

Enderby Band, Midlands Area Champions, at the third section of the national finals, Royal Albert Hall, 1983.

My two uncles, Bernard and Roland, both played, and Mum was the chief fund-raiser, librarian, maker of uniforms. It was a way of life really.

Garry Sleath

Enderby at the Albert Hall

One important event that sticks in my mind is our appearance at the Royal Albert Hall in London. That's got to be the pinnacle. The other is when we did the hat-trick in Corby. When we turned up for the third year, we were in our walking out uniforms. You could see people looking at us and saying 'That's Enderby, Enderby have arrived'. We were the people to beat and when we were there, it was a contest. It's that sort of respect that people have for you as a group, you can't buy it, you have to earn it.

Garry Sleath

Bandsmen go on to great things

Something we are proud of is the number of people who have gone on from the band to do great things. Richard Hallam from Holyoake Street was also taught by my grandfather. He went to the Royal Academy in London, and went on to become musical adviser for Oxfordshire. He has now taken on a government role as an overseer for music education in the country, and was awarded the MBE for his services to music. Roger Harvey is one of the top trombone players after going to Magdalen College, Oxford, and the Manchester School of Music. He went on to be the principle trombonist with the Hallé Orchestra, and also plays in the Philip Jones Brass Ensemble, an elite group of five brass players. He is now co-principal of the BBC Symphony Orchestra, and one of the top trombone players in the country.

Garry Sleath

The story of the Journal

The *Journal* was very much the brainchild of one man, Doug Maas. Doug has served the area as a chiropodist, local politician, and now parish clerk for Narborough. I guess he was one of those people who always had the interests of the local community at heart. He moved to the area in the seventies, on to the Wimpey estate, and didn't really feel part of the community. He came across the *Blaby Courier*, a local community paper with limited circulation, and felt that something like that would serve Enderby and Narborough well. He talked to the people who produced the *Courier*, and found out how it was run, where it was printed, what costs were involved, and began to put a plan together. In 1976, he met Nigel Culver, an apprentice printer who understood the technical side of printing, and between them, they put an advert out looking for 'pioneers' to encourage local people to join them in putting a paper together. They, and their wives, got enough money together to print a short run which they circulated to people they thought might be interested, local businesses, community groups, parish councils, shops, tradesmen. This was well-received, and they recruited a few more people, so that, on 1 May 1976, the first issue of a dozen pages was produced. They counted the houses in the area to receive a copy, five-and-a-half thousand, so that was how many copies were produced.

Graham Anderson

Producing the paper

Originally, the paper was typed using ordinary typewriters, so speed and accuracy were most important. You couldn't edit out mistakes very easily. So we had proper typists, those who earned their living typing, like Gerry Turner, who used to come along on Saturday mornings to layout, and basically type the whole issue flat out. Our current editor, Helen Townsend, joined the *Journal* as a typist some fifteen or twenty years ago. That's how we got the basic copy, but then we had to produce headlines and adverts, which were bigger than normal typeface, by using Letraset, a slow process taking one letter at a time off a plastic sheet and putting it into place. I remember taking four hours to produce one full-page advert for Pratt Brothers. We needed a large group of people to produce the copy, which was then sent to the printer's to be reduced to A3 size. When the sheets came back, they had to be collated by hand. This involved walking along a row of sheets, taking one of each, and then folding the pages by hand to produce a single copy. Very labour intensive! We moved through different advances until at last we came to the age of the personal computer, which meant that several of the processes that had involved lots of people, and had generated a good social atmosphere, now became the work of one person only. This is sad in some ways, because we really enjoyed the social gatherings of the early *Journal* production. For this reason, we haven't taken the technology advances as far as we might have done.

Graham Anderson

Adverts

Once the *Journal* got going, we haven't had to seek advertisers, they have come to us. If you are a local shop, trade or business, you want local custom, and most of our advertisers seem very happy with the response to the adverts we run. We have had stories of people who have had to stop appearing in the journal because they have become swamped with

Journal layout day, November 1990. From left to right: Wesley Cornell, Kathy Hector, Judith Sleath, Marilyn Brackenbury, Helen Townsend.

work as a result of their adverts. A local chiropodist only advertises once every three months now, he has enough work to keep him going. Local builder David Richardson is now almost retired, but he advertised in the very first edition, and still advertises with us. The revenue from advertising is our only source of income – no adverts, no *Journal* – but we have always kept it this way to be completely independent of churches, parish councils and any other outside source.

Graham Anderson

Liaising with the police

We have had quite close links with the police over the years, and I have been able to help them through the paper. When there were two murders in our area, we were able to publish information given to us by the police to appeal to the young folk of the area for further information, and to keep reminding them of the need to ensure their own safety until the culprit was brought to justice.

Graham Anderson

Environmental issues

As a community paper, we are vitally important in providing the community with accurate information about local issues, and this has been particularly important with the issues of the proposed Scottish Power station in

Fun and games in the sand-hole, Sandhill Drive, early 1930s.

Beggars Lane, and the building of the Alliance & Leicester offices on land used by Carlton Hayes Hospital. Large organisations have the money and the power to greatly affect the quality of life of an area, and individuals are weak against them, but informed individuals can band together to have a much greater influence. This is how I see the *Journal* serving the local community.

Graham Anderson

nine
Village Characters

The Spence/Jayes family, c. 1918.

Doctor Berridge

I was born in Moores Lane, in one of a row of small cottages opposite one of the 'yards'. Doctor Berridge lived next door to us. I remember that when he used to visit us, he was a frightening old man. His hands were always freezing cold, I always made him warm them before. He used to extract teeth in his surgery as well. I was terrified of him.

Eileen Briers

Reading the tea leaves

My gran used to live next to the Nag's Head and I used to go there quite a lot while my mum was at work. On a Tuesday afternoon, I used to run home from Townsend Road school because Annie Johnson, who lived where the bank is now with her mother, would come across to my gran's for fortune-telling, to read the tea leaves. I used to rush to get home because I was fascinated by the tea leaves. The lady next door, Ada Vann, would come in, and my gran would get the china tea cups out. They only saw the light of day on a Tuesday afternoon. She'd put the tea pot, milk jug, sugar basin and slop bowl on the table. The table was in the middle of the room, and at the side was the piano, but Annie Johnson never sat on the chair at the table. She always moved the chair and sat on the piano stool. Then it would start. The tea was poured out, they'd drink it, they would empty the slops into the basin, and then Annie would turn the cup over, twist it, and then hold it in her hand. I'd look over her shoulder, and the things she used to tell my gran and Ada would be unbelievable now. My gran would be going on a long holiday – in fact, she never left Enderby! Ada would be going on long journeys, which she never did, but I could never see what she was reading. They would have three cups of tea, then Annie would get up, put the piano stool back under the piano, put the chair back and go down the passage. She wouldn't be outside the front door before my gran would say, 'Oh, Annie does talk a lot of rubbish'. I thought it was the piano stool that made her see in the cups but it wasn't. I was about eight years old at the time.

Christine Bryan

Canon Hibbert

I went to the Church of England at the top of Leicester Lane. There was a vicar there called Mr Hibbert, who was a very nice man. He let us do different things for the church. My husband went into the Church Lads' Brigade.

Sadie Jayes

The tie-seller

One night, about eleven o'clock, the door (of the fish shop) opened, and in walked this dark man. In them days, it was unusual to see a dark man in the village. He'd got a case, and asked if he could show us what he'd got. The shop was full, and he opened this case – he'd got ties, silk scarves and all that, and we bought a scarf from him. It didn't cost a lot, about a shilling, I think. He was a very polite gentleman, and said he had to go, but thanked us for buying from him. He said he wanted to catch the last bus back to Leicester, and wondered why we laughed. We told him the last bus had gone an hour before, and if he wanted to get back to Leicester, he'd have to do the same as anybody else, and walk. I can see that man now, walking down Broad Street, he was a lovely man. This was in the thirties, before the war.

Arthur Cherry

Shaker Moore, the sweep

Years ago everybody had coal fires, so, of course, you had to have your chimney swept. I remember one man who lived up what they called 'backside'. They used to say, 'Oh, you're going to have Shaker Moore do your chimney?' Poor man had the shakes.

Lenny Fawell

Local police

I remember constable 'Bobby' Jesson when we used to go potato picking. Sometimes, we'd go with Blaby Rural District Council, and they would pick us up in the dustcart outside Freddy Spence's newsagents – it was a shoe shop then. Sometimes, we'd go to local farms and travel on pushbikes. Of course, not everyone had a bike, so we'd give some of them a lift on the crossbar, but on the way home, who should be waiting for us by the church but 'Bobby' Jesson. He'd cuff your ear and tell you to get off.

Stuart Buzzard

The midwife and the cushion

Nurse Shercliffe was the local midwife, and was quite a character. She was very deaf and wore a hearing aid. She had a habit of taking it out frequently. She lived in one of the prefabs in Alexander Avenue, and she used to leave a window open with a cushion on it. This was so that if you needed the nurse and she was asleep, you had to throw the cushion at her to wake her up!

Judith North

Film shows at the Co-op

I remember when I was a boy, Mr Gittings, the Co-op boss, used to do film shows in the Co-op Hall for children. You'd pay a copper

Above: *Enderby Co-op committee. From left to right: Mr Cooper, Mr Gittins, Mrs Cooper, Mr Buzzard, Stuart's father, Mr Spence, Joe Smith and Mr Jack Young at the piano.*

Left: *John William Freestone, grandfather of Jenny Smith.*

or two, and you'd come out with a bar of chocolate or something like that. Most of the films were about the Co-op factories and how they made the goods, about the jam factory or the biscuit factory. The Co-op had all their own factories in those days. I suppose they still do because you can still buy Co-op brand biscuits and such like.

G.C.

Grandfather Freestone

I was very close to my grandfather. When I

was a little girl, he used to tell me about his life down Seine Lane, where two of his children were born. He worked for the quarry, and sometimes, when the work ran out, he had to walk over to the quarries at Croft. It didn't matter what the weather was like, rain, hail or snow, he used to have to go if that was where the work was. Life was hard for him. Sometimes, my grandmother hadn't got enough money to feed the family. She had to go to the shop at the top and have a few things 'on the slate', just to last a couple of days. The shop was next door to Langton's Row, opposite the top chapel. At one stage, he was a fireman and worked for the Co-op as well.

Jenny Smith

Danemill to Brockington

Going from Danemill to Brockington was a huge step, especially having to wear uniform. Mr Riley was a terrific P.E. teacher. I remember him teaching me to kick in rugby. I was always a soccer player, and just couldn't get the hang of kicking a conversion in rugby. Mr Riley asked me where I played in the soccer team and I said left wing. He said I should imagine I was crossing the ball, and as soon as he told me that, I was fine, I converted time after time. He always joined in during our lessons. He led by example.

Mark Postlethwaite

Uncle Sam

First of all, Uncle Sam lived on Blaby Road, then just before the war, they bought a shop in West Street, a grocery shop. After he joined up, he went abroad almost straight away. He was in the medical corps. We opened the newspaper one day, and on the front page was a picture of my uncle, tending a wounded

man brought off the battlefield. Uncle Sam was leading the man, who had his eyes bound as if he'd been blinded.

Eileen Briers

No headscarves

I remember once going up to the top chapel with Mrs Turk, the headmaster's wife, who taught art. It was pouring with rain, and a lot of us had headscarves on. As we were going up High Street, Mrs Turk said to one girl 'Take that headscarf off. I'm not walking through the village with a group of people looking like gypsies.' The next day, this girl brought in a picture of the Queen Mother wearing a headscarf. Mrs Turk never said a word!

Christine Bryan

The cat that got the cream

When I worked at Griflex in King Street, we spent a lot of our time in the Dog and Gun where the landlord was a bloke called Bob Cort. His claim to fame was that he was the voice in the advert on television for a type of cream, which talked about the cat that stole the cream. He'd got a pool table in the pub, and we spent a lot of our free time there.

Barry Bryan

A policeman's supper

Our local policeman was Mr Boocock. The police in them days used to walk round the village, and they'd come past the fish and chip shop and put their hand up. That meant they were coming round for their supper. They'd come round the back and into the kitchen. The next thing was my mum and dad taking two lots of supper through. One Friday night,

I was in the bath in the kitchen, we had tin baths in the kitchen in those days. All of a sudden, in walked a policeman and a police-woman. She said, 'I'm very sorry', and I said, 'I should think you are. You'd better go out into the yard while I get a towel round me'. I said to my dad 'You're a right 'un, letting the policewoman catch me in the bath.' PC Boocock was a marvel with anything mechan-ical. One night, he said to my dad, 'Charlie, you're clock's stopped. Give it to me to mend.' My dad said, 'If you can fix that, I'll eat my hat.' I came downstairs next morning and it was working!

Arthur Cherry

Doctor Berridge

Doctor Berridge was the local doctor. He was a stubby little fellow and he had one of them pork-pie hats. He always had a violet flower in his buttonhole. You had to pay for his ser-vices in those days.

Sadie Jayes

A pennyworth of chips!

In those days Mrs Needham took the Brownies, and she lived on Leicester Road. There were two of us lived in the same area, and in the wintertime, we used to like it because, on the way down, she'd call into the chip shop and get a pennyworth of chips for us to eat on the way down in the dark. We weren't allowed to have them in the summer because you couldn't be seen eating chips in the daylight! Unfortunately, she left in 1935 to go and live in Scarborough, so that was the end of the Brownies in Enderby for a while. They started up again, and various people have been involved since Mrs Needham, and they are still going strong today.

Claire Timmins

The scout hut

In the sixties the group grew to three cub packs, two scout troops and a venture unit. Of course, this was before beavers came onto the scene. Parents were very, very dedicated to raising the funds for the new headquarters. I don't know how many tons of newspapers were collected, but I can well remember people like Barry Brown going down night after night bundling newspapers, then on Saturday morning a lorry would arrive and we would load three, four, even five tons of papers on to it. This brought in money, and it also brought in so much support because people could get involved in a money-making scheme which cost them only time. Eventually the scout hut was built on Blaby Road. Maurice Gordon was the driving force behind it, bringing it down from Lancashire and erecting it on the site of the old quarry. The quarry had been filled in with fly ash from Leicester power station and three years later we were building a scout hut on it.

I think one of the memorable tales of that time was that the hut itself was slightly lower than the road, so connecting to the sewers to install toilets for the scouts presented quite a problem. Again, thanks to the dedication of parents and a bit of knowledge of civil engi-neering, the job was done.

John Lane

Granddad and his wood

My granddad was the head gardener at Enderby House. He was mad on chopping firewood. You could see him walking up the street pulling half a tree behind him, and then he'd take it in his shed. He'd stay in the shed all day sawing wood – they had no electric saws in those days. If you went in and asked for some firewood, he'd give you about four little sticks. We used to have to wait until he came out of the shed so we could run in and get enough to light the fire with. He was married twice. He had twenty-one children, ten with one wife, and eleven with the other, and he was only a little man!

Nigel Cooper

Seinepool Cottages

My grandparents lived in Seinepool Cottages, and had so many in the house that they slept downstairs and everyone else slept upstairs in the two bedrooms, head to toe. My Auntie Lily was once getting water from the well there, when the handle swung back and hit her arm. It broke her arm badly. And one of my uncles once fell into one of the pools and got soaked. He daren't go home and show my grandma, so he took his clothes off, put them on sticks and ran up and down the lane trying to dry them.

Jenny Smith

George Freestone and his mother Rhoda outside Seinepool Cottages.

Mr West, the best!

My last class at Danemill was Mr West's. He was by far the best teacher I ever had. He'd been an armourer in one squadron during the war, so with my interest in planes, we connected. I remember, I sat on the front row with a boy called Ian Flynn, and Mr West called me 'Pilot Officer Postlethwaite', and next to me was 'Flight Lieutenant Flynn'. I was always a bit miffed because Ian had a higher rank than me. The great thing about being in Mr West's class was that at the end of the day, we used to queue up at his desk and desperately try to think of a question about the war to ask him. For instance, 'Was your airfield ever strafed during the war?' He'd lean back on his chair, take off his glasses, rub his eyes, stretch, and launch into another half-hour of war stories. I remember one story where he said a bomb landed near him and pinned him against the wall, and his eye popped out of its socket. A medical orderly came along, cleaned around inside and popped it back! I don't know if that story was true, but he certainly was there, and his stories were very vivid. He once brought a piece of Hurricane in and gave it to Flynnie – I was devastated. That's really when I first started drawing planes. I drew a Hurricane and took it in to show him. He really inspired me and gave me encouragement. He was a teacher of the old school.

Everyone at Danemill was scared of Mr West. He would walk round in school assembly while everyone was singing, and if you weren't singing, he'd clip you on the back of the head with a book. But he was also very compassionate. It was while I was in his class

Mark Postlethwaite, local artist, with some of his aviation paintings.

that my father died, and I remember going to him and saying I was sorry that I wasn't in the previous day but my father had died. He was lovely, I saw a different side of him. I was devastated to hear that he died not many years later. I'd love to meet him now and show him what I've achieved since he inspired me to draw planes.

Mark Postlethwaite

Dismantling the motorbike

When I was at the 'big' school, we had a teacher called 'Dog' Hull, who was the science master. He had a 49cc two-stroke motorbike that he used to bring into the class room and allow us to dismantle it. Occasionally, the lads would take bits off the bike and hide them, so that he couldn't get home on it. He didn't wear a crash helmet, but he had a leather flying helmet, and he'd have a scarf wrapped six times round his neck.

Barry Bryan

The midnight butcher

There was a butcher in Enderby who came round every Saturday night with his wagon. He would get the joints of meat out of the back of the wagon and would go round to all the pubs in the village. He was often tipsy, and we'd say to him 'I'll have this piece here' and he'd just chop it up and say, 'Here, have it.' We used to call him the midnight butcher. His name was Mr Robinson.

Lenny Fawell

The sweep

I can remember an old chimney sweep. He lived in the end row in Rawson Street and he'd got an old barrow. Oh, he made such a mess when he swept your chimney! His wife used to come in to see my mother, and she'd stink of soot. You've never seen anything like the mess he made, but people had to have him because there was no-one else.

Sadie Jayes

Dixon of Enderby

The village policeman was called Arthur Dixon, and he was a stern man. I can remember walking past the phone box one night with my dad, and PC Dixon was in the phone box. He'd got his Alsatian with him, it was his pet, not a police dog. We'd been into some mischief a few days before, and got caught down in the cemetery, me and my mates. As soon as I turned the corner by the fish shop and saw Dixon, I thought, 'What's he going to do now?' Anyway, as we going by, my dad said to him, 'Hello, Mr Dixon', so he says, 'Hello, John, I see you've got your lad with you', and nothing more was said. Everybody was strict in those days, so you respected people and you watched what you did.

Barry Bryan

Other local titles published by Tempus

Leicester Voices

CYNTHIA BROWN

These personal memories of the past provide a valuable record of what life used to be like in Leicester. Each story illustrates a different aspect of life in the city as it once was. From memories of childhood and schooldays, work and family, war and peace, each piece offers an oral testimony into the lives of people who have lived in and known Leicester over the decades.
0 7524 2657 5

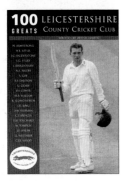

Leicestershire County Cricket Club 100 Greats

DENNIS LAMBERT

Leicestershire County cricket Club has a mercurial history – from its formation in 1879, through the second-class period, promotion to first-class status in 1894 and throughout most of the twentieth century. Despite the initial lack of success, there has always been a wealth of individual talent in evidence and this book is dedicated to 100 of these players, both amateur and professional, whose efforts have given so much pleasure in the past, present and, hopefully, future
0 7524 2175 1

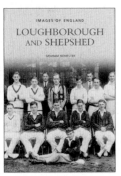

Loughborough and Shepshed

GRAHAM KEMPSTER

This collection of over 180 photographs and other ephemera, drawn from the *Loughborough Echo* archive, traces some of the changes and developments that have taken place in Loughborough and Shepshed during the last 120 years. From Coronation celebrations in 1902 and the construction of Loughborough post office in 1930 to Shepshed Parade and Gala in 1950, each image recalls the social history of the area.
0 7524 3252 4

Nuneaton Volume II

PETER LEE

This absorbing collection provides a nostalgic glimpse into the history of Nuneaton during the last century. Compiled with over 160 photographs and postcards, this selection highlights some of the changes and events that have taken place in the town. From glimpses of working life, including cotton, textiles and engineering industries, through to the modernisation of the town during the 1950s and '60s, each image recalls the social history of Nuneaton.
0 7524 3242 7

If you are interested in purchasing other books published by Tempus, or in case you have difficulty finding any Tempus books in your local bookshop, you can also place orders directly through our website

www.tempus-publishing.com